Real *Indians*

PORTRAITS OF CONTEMPORARY NATIVE AMERICANS

AND AMERICA'S TRIBAL COLLEGES

Real *Indians*

PORTRAITS OF CONTEMPORARY NATIVE AMERICANS

AND AMERICA'S TRIBAL COLLEGES

PHOTOGRAPHS BY ANDREA MODICA

INTRODUCTION BY SHERMAN ALEXIE
INTERVIEWS EDITED BY REBECCA CARROLL
AFTERWORD BY SUZETTE BREWER

PRODUCED BY MELCHER MEDIA, INC., IN ASSOCIATION WITH
THE AMERICAN INDIAN COLLEGE FUND AND WIEDEN + KENNEDY,
WITH GENEROUS SUPPORT FROM THE W.K. KELLOGG FOUNDATION

The American Indian College Fund
8333 Greenwood Boulevard
Denver, CO 80221

Melcher Media, Inc.
124 West 13th Street
New York, NY 10011.

W.K. Kellogg Foundation
One Michigan Avenue East
Battle Creek, MI 49017

First Edition

10 9 8 7 6 5 4 3 2 1

ISBN 0-9717935-1-4

Library of Congress Cataloging-in-Publication Data is on file.

Printed in China

Contents

THIS BOOK IS DEDICATED TO THE HARDWORKING

PEOPLE OF THE TRIBAL COLLEGES WHO HAVE MADE

A LIFELONG AND PERSONAL COMMITMENT TO

CHANGING THE HISTORY OF INDIAN EDUCATION, AND

TO THOSE WHO HAVE RECENTLY PASSED ON TO THE

SPIRIT WORLD: JACK BARDEN, LESTER "JACK" BRIGGS,

DORIS LEADER CHARGE, AND JERRY SLATER.

Real Indians

SHERMAN ALEXIE

I don't know much about photography, or about composition, lighting and framing, or the other wrenches and hammers of the art. And when it comes to the history of photography, I'm only familiar with the famous artists and their work. Heck, I don't know how to change the film in a basic 35-mm camera. When using cameras, I'm a disposable sort of guy. I think the portraits in *Real Indians* are lovely and magical, but I lack the vocabulary to tell you exactly why I think so. I don't have a photographic aesthetic as a picture-taker or picture-watcher. But I am a voyeur with unpredictable obsessions, though I rarely can predict what image or detail will fascinate me. Or maybe I can. Maybe I know exactly what I love to see.

I do admit to having a foot fetish. I can tell you about the bare brown feet of Vernell Lane and Karen Swisher, but I'm disappointed in the overall paucity of bare indigenous feet in this book. I thought Indians were supposed to be barefoot and savage. I guess that's one stereotype broken by *Real Indians*. Maybe we can create a new Native American political slogan: "Indians, if you want to improve your life, put on your shoes!"

I'm trying to be funny because many of these photographs are funny. Some are quietly witty and others are bust-your-gut-and-blow-soda-out-your-nose hilarious. I laughed about Sheila Morris's clean white socks, and I wondered if she bought them especially for the photo shoot. I think her sly smile lets us know she probably got them three-pairs-for-one at Wal-Mart or Target.

Take a look at Vanessa Shortbull's ballet slippers. Can you see the amazing contrast between their white fabric and her brown skin and black hair and eyes, and between a ballerina and the wilderness all around her? And what do you think about the spectacular and ironic beauty of a Native American ballerina? Maybe we need yet another Native American political slogan: "Well, maybe colonialism ain't all bad!"

And go study the warrior-beauty of Tracey Jiloit. She's a crew-cut woman sitting in the middle of a library. A woman-warrior surrounded by books! How many images have you seen of Indian people surrounded by books? Best of all, we can see Jiloit's toes hiding there in the shadows beneath her legs. Have you ever once thought about an Indian woman's toes and their cultural, political, and artistic significance? Do we have any idea about the shape of Crazy Horse's toes? Did Geronimo have cute and chubby toes? And sure, we've all seen a thousand westerns in which Indian people run barefoot across the grassy plains and desert mesas, but have you ever seen a movie in which an Indian woman walks barefoot through a library? Let's make that movie and call it "Yo, Indian girls and boys, books will save your lives!"

Of course, I'm asking you to scrutinize these Indians, and that's nothing new, because we Indians have been scrutinized for the last five centuries. Every one of us is a twenty-four-hour tourist attraction, indigenous fun house, spiritual roller coaster, and living museum. We get stopped by obsessed AmerIndiophiles in airports and restaurants, and curious little white kids chase us down city streets while screaming, "It's an Indian! It's an Indian!" Disenchanted white Christians have turned Jesus into a New Age Navajo who likes Sioux sweat lodges and Cherokee crystals. Turn on your television right now and flip through your two hundred channels of the good and bad, and I guarantee you'll see at least twenty Indians, all dressed in feathers and beads.

It's 2003 and Indians are still exotic! But that exoticism is only about the surface image. Our true exoticism, our mystery, is much deeper. It's sad to have to reiterate an obvious point, but Indians are human beings engaged in complicated human relationships. A few of these photographs hint at those complex relationships. Take a look at Elden Lawrence, a brush-cut bear of a man, holding the hand of a child whose face remains off-camera. Who is the kid? Or notice how Janine Pease-Pretty On Top holds a child who plays peekaboo with the camera. Who is that little girl? Are the picnic basket and bucket on the ground for berry picking? Dr. Pease-Pretty On Top is the first Crow woman to receive her doctorate, so let's celebrate the Ph.D. who likes to berry-pick! And who is the guy in the field behind Dennis Bercier? Does he sing with Dennis Bercier? I discovered the mysterious man is Bercier's son. Does he sing with his father, or does he like to hover in the background and listen?

For me, two of the more mysterious and evocative photographs are of Benjamin Barney and David Risling. Now, we Indians are so often portrayed as spiritual beings, as wise men and women who need sponges to soak up all of the wisdom seeping out of our pores. And Barney and Risling certainly appear to be wise men. Barney kneels as if in prayer, and Risling's face and long gray hair would not be out of place in an Edward Curtis pictography. But these two photographs also play with stereotypical images and emotions. Barney tenderly holds what must be an important object to him (I can't tell what it is), but notice the overturned bucket reflecting light and the garden hose snaking through the dust. I would guess the photographer carefully placed the bucket and hose, but they still look messy and disorganized. Can you be wise and disorganized? Can you be messy and spiritual? The hose and bucket feel like contradictions, like conflicts, like anachronisms. The picture seems to be asking me a question I can't quite understand. And what about the mesa reflected in the window above Barney? As we look at a photograph of a reflection of a mesa, are we two or three times removed from the earth? And tell me, Mr. Barney, what the heck are you holding in your hands? Would you tell me if I asked you in person? Or shall we let the mystery be?

When I first glanced at Risling's portrait, I thought he was leaning against a tree. But then I noticed he was holding a woman's hand. And then I noticed he was holding the hand of a brown-skinned woman who stood above him. Maybe Risling is holding the hand of a tree, of a powerful Indian woman that could be his wife or his girlfriend or his sister or his aunt or his daughter. Who is she? I don't really want to know. But I learned that Risling holds his wife's hand, and she's white! The woman's shadowed skin and my unconscious racism fooled me into thinking she's Indian. I apologize. And I love that an Indian man sits beneath a woman, white or Indian. Is this portrait a comment on the power of the matriarchy? Or is it more of a testament to the power of love between men and women? There's no doubting some kind of love story is happening in Risling's portrait, and doesn't he look happy and smart and pleased and yes, wise!

Don't Barney and Risling look like holy men? And check out their biographies, one man a college professor and the other often described as the father of Indian education in California. So, in fact, these two guys are college-educated wise men. And then you add in Les Northrup, a college professor wearing his academic gown and cap while standing in the trees, and you've got three wise men! What would Edward Curtis think of that?

Everyone in *Real Indians* is wise, but it's a literary wisdom. These smart men and women are bookish and probably a little geeky. Let's celebrate a book filled with indigenous nerds and their eccentric styles! Flip through the pages and count how many men wear their hair long. Not very many. What are we supposed to do with shorthaired Indians? How do we classify Indian men in suits and ties? And what should we say about the Indian women with their curly hair? Can a reservation hairstylist also be a sacred figure? Now, certainly there are men and women who wear their hair as Indians have traditionally worn it, long and wild or long and braided, and dang, they make it look good. Take a look at handsome Ron McNeil, great-great-great-grandson of Sitting Bull, sitting on that Harley with his hair blowing in the breeze. Doesn't he make you lonely for 1872? And what about the beautiful Agnes Kenmile sitting with her deer hides? I'll bet she knows the lyrics and music of a thousand tribal songs. Wouldn't you love to sit at her feet and listen to her sing about six hundred and twelve of them? And, using the same tone of voice, wouldn't you want to ask Jim Shanley about his golf handicap?

Yes, take a look at the wondrous and surprising details that contradict everything you thought you knew about Indians. Notice the boxing gloves, baseball hats, Nike sandals, khaki pants, muscle cars, fly-fishing poles, flower-print dresses, comfortable European shoes, basketballs and hoops, mountain bikes, videotapes, and barbecue cookers. Look at all of these Native-Americans successfully living on both sides of the hyphen!

But, hey, why are you listening to me? I don't know anything about photography, and I know less about these real Indians. Go spend a few minutes with their faces and a few more minutes with their stories. These Indians, and all other Indians, are not who you think they are. They're not even who they think they are. Every Indian in this book is a mystery, and you're going to have a good time trying to figure them out.

Marita Hinds

TESUQUE PUEBLO
MAJOR GIFTS OFFICER,
IAIA DEVELOPMENT OFFICE,
INSTITUTE OF AMERICAN INDIAN ARTS
SANTA FE, NEW MEXICO

JADE IS THE OLDEST, SHE'S ON MY LEFT, AND SHE'S TWELVE. Cienna is seven. Jade's father has two other daughters from a previous marriage and their names are Amber and Crystal, so we wanted to use another stone name. With Cienna, I had heard that name years ago and it always stuck in my head. I thought it was pretty, and it reminded me of the color sienna, but I spell it with a C.

I guess this image is evocative of a traditional storyteller. Usually it's a grandmother telling her grandchildren stories, and they're seated around her or on her lap. Often the children fall asleep. So this is me with my girls, and their eyes are closed as if they had fallen asleep during a storytelling. Much has happened in our family and our different lives that lends itself to storytelling. When we're down at the powwow at my aunt's house, cooking and eating, we all sit at the table and tell stories and laugh for hours.

My daughters are the main thing in my life. We do practically everything together, and I'm constantly aware that whatever I do affects them. Many of my decisions are based on them, but it's wonderful. I'm a single parent raising two girls, and we have a great relationship.

Certainly art runs in our family. I'm both an artist and an arts administrator. Cienna dances ballet and Jade's a painter. My father was a painter and my brother, Mark, is a sculptor. A friend of the Pueblo, Norman E. Hinds, adopted my father out of the village when he was a child and, seeing my father's talent early on, put him through art school in California. Later, my father went to the Art Institute of Chicago, where he met my mom. They moved to California, and my dad pursued a career as an artist. Mark and I were brought up going to art shows and openings with him, and also attending the Santa Fe Indian Market put on by the Southwestern Association for Indian Arts, where I used to work.

I'm more involved as an arts administrator than as an artist, but if I won the lottery and had the chance to work on my own art more, I would. When you have children, though, you have to work to pay the bills. And I love my job. I enjoy coming to work and supporting other artists. Although I do wonder what it would be like to concentrate on my own art. The lottery was high the other day, so I'm going to go buy a ticket.

We moved from the Bay Area to Santa Fe when I was nine. It was perfect timing, too, because this whole movement of Indian artists was just beginning to emerge, and so my dad was at the forefront of Native arts. Also, I think what was going on in Berkeley at the time was another reason to leave California. It was the late 1960s, and there were a lot of the riots and demonstrations going on near our home. My dad felt that he wanted to raise us in a safer environment.

Santa Fe had real neighborhoods with lots of kids and we just felt safe. During the summer, we would visit the Pueblo all the time, and we knew that eventually we would move here. All our cousins were here, and all our friends from the summer. We were always at the Pueblo for ceremonies and feast days, so when we finally did move, it wasn't much of a transition. Sadly, we didn't move until 1975, a year after my father passed away.

My mother is an only child from New York, and I think when my father died, she could have easily packed us up and gone back to New York. But she knew that my father had wanted us to experience the Pueblo culture and tradition, especially since we hadn't had that when we were younger. And that's one of the main reasons it's so important to me that my girls are immersed in the culture. Since I wasn't really brought up with it until we moved here, I have had a lot of things explained to me. When I was fourteen and started dancing at the Pueblo, I always wondered why certain things were done and what they meant. With my daughters, it has all been taught from day one. It's an integral part of their lives, and will be with them forever.

Juan Perez

KLAMATH AND MODOC

STUDENT LIFE AND ATHLETICS COORDINATOR
AND ALUMNUS, SALISH KOOTENAI COLLEGE
PABLO, MONTANA

MY DAUGHTER, OLIVIA, IS NINETEEN MONTHS OLD. I WOULD have liked for my wife to be in the portrait, too, but she had to work. My family is very important to me. Everything else in my life revolves around them. It means a great deal to me that I provide for my daughter and my wife, and that I do things with them. My wife and I are expecting our second child in a few weeks. Olivia will have a baby brother or sister soon. We don't know what we're having yet. We both feel that one of the most exciting aspects of having a child is the surprise of finding out whether it's a boy or a girl when it's born.

My mother lives next door, partly because I feel it's important to have grandparents close by. I remember things about my grandma and grandpa from my childhood, even though they passed away when I was still a young boy. I think their death left an impact on my life—there is a certain kind of love that grandparents give that's different from the kind parents give. Besides, my mom was always bugging me about when I was going to make her a grandma, and so my wife and I brought her here a few days before Olivia was born—I wanted her to see the birth of my daughter.

I grew up in Portland, Oregon, around alcoholism and occasional violence in my house. I didn't want that for me, and I knew I didn't want it for my kids. I always knew that I wanted to have children, but I also wanted to make sure that I was ready when I did. I wanted to be certain that I had a secure job and that I was able to care for them. My brother, Silas, and I were both brought up with the knowledge that we would take care of our families.

Silas is two years older. As boys, we did everything together. When I first moved to Montana from Portland, I stayed with him. At the time, he was an emergency foster parent. Seeing the way he cared for the kids who were placed with him made me realize how much I admire him. He has eight children now. Three of them are adopted—girls who were his foster children for probably eight years before he was finally able to adopt them.

I've followed my brother in a lot of ways. Education wasn't really pushed in my family or in my immediate environment. I think my high school probably graduated me just to get rid of me. When Silas joined the military, I joined the military. After he moved up here to Montana, I moved up here. And when he went to college, I felt that if he could do it (he had dropped out of high school, taken the GED, and continued on to get a bachelor's degree) then I could do it. In the fall of 1996, I enrolled in college. I was twenty-seven.

I knew that I wanted to work with at-risk kids and that I could do that through the Human Services program. I had a counselor in high school who was always on my side, even though I liked to get in trouble. Not trouble with the law or anything, but I skipped school, slacked off academically, and I probably partied more than I should have. This counselor was always there to give me support when I needed it, and it made me feel good that there was an adult who didn't give up on me. I wanted to be able to do the same thing for other kids. And I also felt that I could be a good Indian male role model—to show kids that not all Indian men are bad.

I didn't grow up with tribal culture and neither did my wife—her father was adopted into a white family. We're both learning a lot, just as Olivia is. There are elders who speak Salish to her, and I think being around the tribe will help her to learn about respect and the importance of community. Olivia loves to powwow dance. From the time she was six months old in her walker, she was out in the dance arbor dancing and running around. Someday she'll be one of the people who will help to keep her tribe alive.

David Risling

HOOPA VALLEY, KARUK, AND YUROK

COFOUNDER, D-Q UNIVERSITY, AND FORMER
DIRECTOR AND PROFESSOR OF NATIVE AMERICAN
STUDIES, UNIVERSITY OF CALIFORNIA-DAVIS
DAVIS, CALIFORNIA

MY WIFE, BARBARA, AND I HAVE BEEN MARRIED FIFTY-EIGHT years. We both went to Hoopa Indian School, and that's the school that my dad took over, the first Indian school taken over from the federal government in 1931. It's not in any history books, but it's in the archives. It wasn't called the Indian school at that time, just the Hoopa Valley High School. When I graduated in 1939, Barbara was in the tenth grade. We were only halfway high school sweethearts, though. Barbara says there were others.

When I first went to school, nobody was allowed to speak an Indian language. We got beat up if we did, and we were just little kids. We had to do everything but be an Indian. That was my first four years, and that's when my dad stepped in and said he'd had enough of this stuff. He only finished the second grade himself before he ran away from all the boarding schools. So he got together with some of the people that agreed with him, and they took over the school.

I don't speak my language now, because I've been away for years and years, but I can understand some of it. See, I was born Yurok, which was part of the Hoopa Reservation for a long time until the two separated, and the Hoopa moved up north. And then, the two languages became about as far apart as you could get in languages. I used to understand Yurok when I was little, but when we moved up to Hoopa, all the kids would make fun of me because I couldn't speak well. And my dad spoke another language, too, Karuk, and so that's three completely different languages.

When I was a boy, my dad brought me into the woodshed and told me, "You're going to go off to college." I said, "Yeah," though I didn't even know what college really was. He asked me what I was going to take there, and I had no idea that you had to take something. Then he made a little dot in the center of a big circle on the ground, and he asked me what it was, and I said a dot and a circle. He said, "Well, you're right, but I want to show you what a wheel has to run on." And then he asked me what would I like to do. I had never even thought about that, so finally I said I wanted to be a lawyer, because he always had these lawyers and congressmen and everybody else chasing him around. And he said, "You think that wheel will run with one spoke?"

He explained that Indians were only about 1 percent of the population, the dot in the center, and the dominant society was the circle. He said we may have to live in the dominant society, but we are still Indian people. And he went down the line and told me what was important. The first thing was who you are—your spirituality. Then the second thing he talked about was education. He went on about a whole number of things, and about how you have to write your own history, because the history that's written is false. And he told me, don't bother to come home if you forget who you are. Don't forget who you are and if you start something, you finish it. You know, a lot of people, when it gets too hot, they quit. What he was getting at is that you have to learn how to put all the spokes together in order for the wheel to turn.

There are a lot of changes coming out by Indian people. A long time ago, all these government people thought they knew everything, but they don't have any of the facts. The big thing that I'm happy about is that all over the country, people are beginning to be who they are, and they can live in two worlds. That's what I did. I was on ships. I was in Congress. I can go just about any place on the white man's side and be his friend. And on the Indian side, I get invited to almost every tribe in the United States, and they know who I am. I belong to about every Indian organization in the country that has power.

You can live in the two worlds. And that was what my dad was saying: "Get to know both worlds and put all the spokes together."

Vanessa Shortbull

OGLALA LAKOTA
FORMER STUDENT, OGLALA LAKOTA COLLEGE,
AND ALUMNA, UNIVERSITY OF SOUTH DAKOTA
RAPID CITY, SOUTH DAKOTA

TO TELL YOU THE TRUTH, I LAUGH WHEN PEOPLE SAY, "YOU'RE Miss South Dakota. You must've been at the top of your high school class." Well, no. When I was in high school, the only reason I planned on going to college was so that I could be a ballet performance major. And then, one day, my teacher said to me, "What happens if you break your leg or you hurt your back dancing?" I'd never even thought of that. She encouraged me to go into political science, because I loved to talk and had an interest in government.

I enrolled at the University of Utah as a dance performance major, and I also started taking some political science courses. But I wasn't happy there, so I came back home and went to Oglala Lakota College (OLC) for a year and a half before going on to the University of South Dakota, where I am currently attending. I think what I enjoyed most about being at a tribal college was the sense of community. OLC was a stepping-stone for me, and it gave me the confidence to be vocal and to get involved. I was president of the OLC Democrats, and I was active in the Political Science League. My time at OLC gave me a sense of duty, and the poise to go further outward into the world.

I love the political scene and I want to work on campaigns and get people out to vote, because I think the system can work and does work if you have the right mindset. People say, "You're Indian, so you must have anti-government feelings and sentiments." And I say, "We can't just say we hate the government and expect it to change for us." You can talk tribal sovereignty all you want, but . . . you can't expect politicians to care if you don't get out and vote.

The problem is not so much registering people to vote, because I think you can get people to care. It's actually making the polls easy for people to get to. In the 2000 election, I was driving kids from our dorm to the central voting place, this huge armory in Clay County, because I knew there was no way they were going to walk there. People were traveling thirty miles just to vote. That is ridiculous.

All this unified patriotism resulting from September 11th is almost like a slap in the face when you look at the primary results—people are still not voting. The tyrants who flew the planes into the World Trade Center come from a place where they don't even have open elections. We can put flags on our cars, go to Wal-Mart, and buy decorations for our houses to show how patriotic we are, and yet we can't go out for three minutes and vote. It makes me want to scream.

When people ask me what I want to be doing in five years, I tell them that I just live each day as much as I can and meet new opportunities as they come. I do plan on going to law school, and I'd love to hold a position in public office someday, but never in my wildest dreams did I imagine I'd be doing stand-up comedy in an NBC performance studio in New York City.

I had a talent search audition in Denver on September 11 of 2001. I never thought that I would have to go through with a performance with all the stuff that was happening outside. The producer holding the auditions was from NBC in New York. I remember him being so angry that somebody had had the nerve to come into his city and expect the world to stop. He gave this speech that gave me goose bumps, and I thought, "You know what? The world will go on. Tomorrow will be another day. It'll be a changed world, but it will go on." And then he said, "Contestant number one?"

I was going to do a dramatic monologue, but then I remembered my grandmother telling me over and over that Indian people have a great sense of humor—we laugh to keep from crying. Whenever I'd done public speaking before, thinking that I was being really inspiring and motivational, people always told me that I was actually funny and that my life is hilarious. So I got up there and just told these stories. The producer sent me to the semi-finals in Syracuse, then to the finals in New York City, where I got the chance to audition for *The Sopranos*. I didn't get the part, but the opportunity was something I would have never imagined possible.

My mom has always said that I can do anything in the world that I want to. I can be a nurse or a mechanic or a senator. I can do all these things in my life, and I think that's how your life should be. You can do as many things as you put your mind to.

Dr. Lanny Real Bird

CROW

DIRECTOR, LEARNING LODGE INSTITUTE,
LITTLE BIG HORN COLLEGE
CROW AGENCY, MONTANA

AS A YOUNG KID, I ATTENDED TRIBAL CEREMONIES AND THE elders would make me help out. This is how I learned cultural knowledge—from being a worker, a servant to the services and preparations of ceremonies. I was a student of the traditional education—get wood, set up lodges and tipis, gather different medicines, prepare medicines, collect water, help others who are doing preparation, and find means to help.

Students of traditional knowledge had no right to express any opinions, even if sometimes we might have felt uncomfortable doing the work. If we didn't do as we were told, or we questioned anybody, we were scolded. So we just minded our business and listened and did what was asked of us.

My biological father gave me to his brother, who then raised me in the tradition of the Crow. He was my uncle but I called him my natural father, and he raised me in these ceremonial ways while my biological father exercised his other responsibilities. He was the leader of the tribe, and he needed to commit himself to serving the people. Many times in Crow tradition, when a man is selected to serve as a war chief or a leader, he gives away his children to be raised properly by others, because his commitment must be to the community.

My natural father would take me to sweats, and sometimes I'd be in these ceremonies and wake up and people would be praying for me. I can remember a few instances when people who are not with us in this world were there wishing that I would become a doctor, and so I thought maybe these people wanted me to be some kind of physician. I only understood their good wishes, because I knew that they loved me.

I received a scholarship from the University of North Dakota to study premedicine, and I got on a cross-country team there. But I didn't last too long because I wasn't used to that system. Nobody told me or prepared me for this culture shock that I would experience.

I finally ended up getting my degree in business at Eastern Montana College. I changed my major five times—from premed to business to psychology to engineering and then back to business. I returned to business because I was on this engineering scholarship at Eastern, but my financial aid credits were about to expire, and so I thought the only feasible way to accomplish a degree was through business.

I came back to the rez, and at that time, there was a whole bunch of chaos in the tribal government, and nobody wanted to take these administrative positions over there. Being right out of college, a crazy guy, green and everything, I said I could do it. And they dumped everything on me—all of the tribe's financial management—and I learned how to be the finance manager, right on the job.

I've since learned that in the tribal colleges, you don't wear just one hat. I became a math instructor in the preparatory areas, and then there were voids in other departments where instructors were needed—computers, science, business, English, and all across the board. I could say that I probably taught in every department here at the college from then until now.

A few years later, at a traditional ceremony, one of the elders said to me in Crow, "Son, why don't you go get a master's and we'll see what it's all about?" When you're in a ceremony, you watch what you say, and when you present something, it's formal. We don't really put people on the spot in these ceremonies, but if you're put on the spot by one of the elders, you don't say no. My father, who was sitting about four people away, looked at the others, and said, "None of us has a master's. We'll help you do this."

It wasn't my goal, you know, but at the same time, when they started praying about it, things started getting holy. I went to Montana State University and got my master's and an education doctorate.

Marvin B. Weatherwax

BLACKFEET

DEPARTMENT CHAIR, BLACKFEET STUDIES,
BLACKFEET COMMUNITY COLLEGE
BROWNING, MONTANA

I NEVER LEARNED TO SPEAK ENGLISH UNTIL I WAS EIGHT years old. My grandfather taught me. I went to school when I was seven, and I could only speak a few words of English. The teacher had us get up in front of the room the first day of school and tell everyone what we did for the summer. I got up there—I could say "swim" and "ride" and a few other words—and one of the kids began to harass me, so I started saying stuff in Blackfeet language. My teacher got very upset and she told me, "You can't speak Indian here." Then she took a rod from the chalkboard about two and a half inches wide, an inch thick, and a foot long, and she hit my knuckles with that rod, and it broke my knuckles on one side. So I decided that wasn't the place for me.

I got on my horse and rode home. When I told my grandfather what happened, he lost his cool. He got in his buggy and drove down to the school, and I came with him. As soon as he was in the school, that teacher must've seen it in his eyes or something, because she headed out. He chased her around and told her he was going to break her arms because she broke my knuckles. But he couldn't catch her, and so he stopped and said, "I'm going to teach him at home because you guys are too mean. Maybe I'll let him come back next year."

My grandparents raised me from birth—I was born in their home. I was premature and I only weighed a couple of pounds. It was October and a big snowstorm was coming. Our potatoes were still in the field, and they had to get the spuds out of there. My mom was seven months pregnant, and she was helping my grandparents harvest the potatoes, and that caused her to have me early. Because of the snowstorm, I never got to see a doctor until I was over a month old. When I finally saw the doctor, he told my grandparents and my mom that I would be very lucky if I lived to be two months old. So my grandfather, he was a medicine man, asked my mom if he could have me. She said yes, if he could get me to live. So he adopted me and raised me as his own child. While I was growing up, my parents were more like my aunt and uncle.

After high school, I was drafted and went to Vietnam. I was there a little under a year before I was captured. There was one other soldier who was captured with me. This is what happened.

There were four Americans being held prisoner—my buddy and me, and two other Americans, two black guys from another unit. They hung us by our arms along this wall. They come by and asked the first guy what unit he was from, how many were in his unit, and where his unit was at, and the first guy spit on them and started cussing them out. So they cut him with a knife from kidney to kidney. The same thing happened to the second guy and the third guy. I was the last one on the end, and I was thinking, "My gosh, what am I going to do?" I didn't want to die, but I couldn't very well tell them anything.

So when they came to me, I told them everything they wanted to know, only it was in the Blackfeet language, and that's what saved me from getting cut and killed. They tried to figure out what I was saying and they worked on me just about every day trying to decipher the language. I was a POW for three years, eight months, and twenty-seven days, and the whole time I spoke nothing but the Blackfeet language. They did all kinds of things to get me to speak English. They'd stick things through my hands and my feet and through my tongue and cheeks. They pulled off my fingernails and toenails. Stuff that could probably kill people, but I just completely put pain out of my mind. I refused to feel pain. They asked me the same questions over and over again and I always gave the same answers. To this day, I always say that my language kept me alive. I credit my Blackfeet language for my life.

Dr. Elden Lawrence

SISSETON-WAHPETON SIOUX
FORMER PRESIDENT AND ALUMNUS,
SISSETON WAHPETON COLLEGE,
FKA SISSETON WAHPETON COMMUNITY COLLEGE
SISSETON, SOUTH DAKOTA

WHEN I WAS PRESIDENT AT SISSETON WAHPETON Community College, I emphasized to our director the importance of getting students started with gardening, rather than having them jump right into big livestock or farming operations. Because the more you know about the basics of farming, the better chance you have of being successful at it. There's nothing like getting out in the garden and finding out if you even want to do the work that it takes, and then learning what it's like to plant a seed and have it grow into something.

When I was a kid, my dad always had a good-sized garden. We were a big family, and we all had to work in the garden because at that time we had no commodities, very little work available, and no welfare. So you had to raise a lot of your own food if you were going to keep from starving. We also had root cellars and stored a lot of stuff in there for the winter—never enough to last through the whole winter, but it would get us through part of it, and then of course we hunted wild game.

My great-grandfather, Lorenzo Lawrence, was a farmer. He lived during the 1862 Dakota Conflict, and was one of the very first Indian farmers. He learned from the missionaries, and I don't know if he enjoyed farming that much, but he knew it was a way to take care of his family. He raised livestock and potatoes and corn to keep his household supplied, and tribes shared with one another, too. So my history with farming and gardening goes back at least to him and has been passed down through the generations. For me, gardening comes naturally.

Up until about the 1830s, the Dakota were a hunting and gathering culture. There were no gardening projects that I know of, but there were plenty of wild berries, plants, roots, and game to sustain them. And when the trading came in, they started to modernize a little bit more and were able to develop a small industry by getting furs and exchanging them with the fur traders for things that made their life a little bit easier.

I was born in 1936, during the Depression era, and my earliest recollections were of hard times. Being farmers, both my father and grandfather were hit hard by the Depression and never fully recovered. I've never known what it is to be affluent or well off because by the time I was born everything was pretty much gone. But I do know that at one time my grandfather, and my father when he was young, had a lot of horses and modern machinery, which for that time was all horse drawn. My family had a pretty good life up until about the 1920s or so; the Depression and the fall of the stock market may not have affected us directly, but indirectly it affected everybody.

I retired as president of Sisseton Wahpeton at the end of June 2002, and it was a traumatic change for me because, just prior to that, the college had been provided with expansion funds and so we had a lot of construction projects going on. My days were filled with people coming in and out of my office wanting answers and decisions, and there were meetings with the various committees that we had. Sometimes I would be on my way out and get stopped several times before I even got to the door. And then, suddenly all of that was gone. I wake up in the morning and there's no place to go and no schedule, no nothing, and it took a while to get used to that. I'm still getting used to that.

It had reached a point at my job where I couldn't relax. I would try to work in the garden when I came home, but it wasn't enjoyable and it didn't make sense to me. It felt like I was wasting my time. I was thinking more about working on a million-dollar project or a grant that would bring in money for the college. That seemed more important than getting a few weeds out of the garden. But now, one thing that has helped me with this transition is putting up my own hay and working the land with my son-in-law. He has another job, but his days are long, and so I can do other things until he comes home at night and helps with the haying. I think it has helped me to reestablish my sense of self.

Dennis Bercier

TURTLE MOUNTAIN BAND OF CHIPPEWA
NORTH DAKOTA STATE SENATOR AND ALUMNUS,
TURTLE MOUNTAIN COMMUNITY COLLEGE
BELCOURT, NORTH DAKOTA

SINGING IS MEDITATIVE. I DON'T REALLY CARE FOR THE WORD "chanting." It's like using the word "American Indian" or "Native American"—it sounds so patronizing. Just call me Indian. Maybe that's wrong, but I've lived with it all my life and it seems to work just fine.

Playing my drum and singing feels like the revitalization of my ties to Indian culture and the renewal of my children's spirits. It's a humbling experience, even if I may not be the best singer. It's kind of like regeneration. Sometimes when I'm halfway through a song, I will remember some of the powwows and ceremonies that I've been to and the people who were there and who have been instrumental in helping me to become more aware of who I am as a tribal person.

The songs and memories are like vignettes. They only last a few seconds, but it feels like you're in the memory for longer, reexperiencing the feeling of being taught by an elder or of singing to your child at their first ceremony. It all goes through you really quickly, but it feels good. Some of these songs are hundreds of years old, and there's no book of sheet music. They are passed down through the generations, and singing them is about pride, honor, and remembrance.

The biggest struggle for Indians has been to keep our identity. There have been attempts to starve it out of us, and to get rid of it through boarding schools and wars. But we are holding fast, and for many tribes, the drum is at the center of tribal identity. It symbolizes several things, but one thing it symbolizes is the heart.

The drum is circular and so it also represents the cycle of life— being reborn, coming around through your teens and adulthood, your elderly position in life, and then back to the ground. For the most part, the drum is considered female, and so the circle also represents the womb. The sound of the drum is the heartbeat of tribal people all over the world.

The Big Drum Society among the Chippewa was started during the middle 1800s. In fact, there's a story about that. A Sioux lady was hiding in some reeds because at that time the Chippewa and the Sioux Tribes were at war. As she prayed, the Creator looked down on her and told her that he was going to give her something that she could use as a peace offering to end the warring. He gave her songs, a few sticks, and a drum. She brought them to the center of a big field, and a couple of Chippewa people sat down around her, along with a couple of Dakota. She offered the drum and they all started singing, and soon there was no more warring. Some say stories like these are just folklore, but they often speak a lot of truth.

Indians are a visionary people in many ways. Tribal people went to war for America even when we were not considered its citizens. We were not treated as human beings, yet we fought for this country, the one that took all of our land. Indian people, I think, have always known what is right. Nobody wants war, but we are able to see things while they are still in their very faint stages. We know when something is going to have a certain impact, so we take action. Other people may say, "Is that some kind of magic or something?" It's not. It's just that tribal people tend to be more closely attached to things that are going on in their natural environment.

There's a spirit in everything. Everything has a purpose and a place. There are times when I just close my eyes and sing, as if in a trance, and it's almost like being on automatic pilot. The vocals kind of just roll out with their highs and lows. It's so peaceful. Now, if you try to force yourself onto a drum, the drum will always teach you humility. You'll start too early. You'll end too late. But all that means is that the drum is reminding you that you're a human being. You make mistakes just like everyone else.

The drum will always be patient with you. It will say, "Okay, I can wait. You've got family to take care of, you have an elder to take care of. You've got other things that take priority. I will always be here." And if you take care of the hides in the meantime, when you come back the drum is there for you and nothing has changed.

Benjamin **Barney**

NAVAJO

DIRECTOR, CENTER FOR DINÉ TEACHER
EDUCATION, DINÉ COLLEGE
CHINLE, ARIZONA

IN THE LATE '80S, AFTER MANY YEARS IN ACADEME, I LEFT it entirely to herd sheep for two years. I wanted to go back to the reservation and experience the world I came from before it was too late. So that's what I did. I tried to live without money, to live without vehicles, to live by the seasons, to live by living with sheep.

During that two-year period, I read close to seven books a week. Sometimes I read to myself, sometimes out loud to the sheep. I read classics, the Bible, Hindu literature. And I realized: I know this culture that I grew up with, the Navajo and the English languages. I have lessons to teach. Not long after that, I sold all my sheep.

I wanted to go to a place where I wasn't familiar with the politics, the government, or the jobs; where there were no relatives. I ended up in southern Germany. There, I would wake up in the mornings, lie in my bed on the floor, and think to myself, "Now I have to make a decision. I must know why I have to wake up, why I have to go out, because if I have to get up, I'm getting up to go somewhere." You do things in your work or within a community, but if you don't have that structure, why do you get out of bed? And one morning, as I'm doing all this meditative thinking, a person appeared to me.

I was lying in my bed and this person appeared in front of me, and we had a conversation. He told me that I had created him, and that whatever I think, do, dream, wish, or want, wherever I want to go, he is ahead of me. He's the one who tells me which way to go, who to be friends with, who to love.

After he left, I thought about what had happened, and then later, my whole religious belief system vanished. My sense of family and of all my relatives completely disappeared. I didn't miss anything Native American or Navajo.

I took a long walk nearby in the Black Forest, as I often would, just taking one step after another. I had walked for a long time before I sat down on a bench. It was really quite nice, and as I sat, there was a shimmering tree in the light. I think it was a birch. And as I looked at the tree with the sunlight on it, I thought of beauty, and this person reappeared. I had another conversation with him, but this time I noticed that he was a white person. He was not Indian; his hair was blond, not black. His skin was white, not brown. I wanted to see his face, but he had no face and no eyes. No distinct nose or mouth. I said to him, "You don't have any eyes, mouth, or nose." And he said, "It's true I don't have a face, because you never gave me a face." And immediately I understood that over the years this had become a central issue in my life—Navajo people have such a strong set of facial features and you can't manipulate or play with them.

That was the last time I saw him, in 1992. I decided to call him Prince because he was like somebody you want to be and who then begins to dictate your actions. According to Gandhi and much religious literature, if you follow the dictates of somebody else, you're not alive. And it's the same with Navajo thought: it's not worth living through someone else, because then it's not you doing the living. I don't think this process of understanding is about trying to become something other than what you are; for me, it was something that I had to do before I could continue on with my life.

When I came back to the reservation after that time in Germany, I understood that as a Native American, however you define yourself, it's not about racial color. It doesn't mean a certain set of criteria to be determined and maintained. It's about opening your mouth and making sounds. You have a choice over that, and total authority and power. Call it Navajo, English, German, or French, but you produce it yourself, and that is, in many ways, what culture is.

Carly **Kipp**

BLACKFEET

ALUMNA, BLACKFEET COMMUNITY COLLEGE
BROWNING, MONTANA

I WAS JUST, LIKE, THIS BIG NERDY GIRL GROWING UP. I drew and studied and rode horses, and when I was really little, I beat up all the boys so none of them liked me. I used to ride all the time. I'd get up every morning and go out to be with the horses. If they were sleeping, I'd go talk to them, put their heads in my lap, and gently wake them up. I had this one really cool horse—a pinto—and she was real smart and sassy. I remember the first time I got on her she just took off with me. Her name was Wahine, which means "lady" in Hawaiian.

As I got a little older, I lost weight playing ball and got kind of cute, I guess. There was this boy in school who was a year older than me, and he wanted to be my boyfriend. I was like, "What's that all about?" I'd never even kissed a guy. I was fifteen. I had no idea. He raped me and I didn't know what to do.

The first person I told about the rape was my best friend—my older sister—and she didn't really say anything. Then the next day I told one of my friends at school, and she was ready to fight. She was going to tell this guy off, but he told her and everybody else in high school that I was just a drunk and a whore. This was in September, so it was the first month of school. That kind of sewed up my reputation in high school. I had never even kissed a guy, and all of a sudden I was labeled a whore. About six months after that, I was raped again by some guys at a party, and then about a month after that, my older sister started dating the guy who raped me the first time. She was with him for four years.

I thought I'd be in trouble if I told my parents, and I didn't want to ruin anything for my sister, so I didn't say anything. I just started getting into my artwork and doing things by myself. They thought I was into drugs or something. The next thing you know, all the attention, which had never been on me, was on me, and that really stressed me out. I decided to leave, which was a bad decision, but not all bad because I learned a lot.

I ran away to Los Angeles and met this man. He beat me up for, like, three years. When I turned eighteen, I realized that I didn't have to be there anymore. So I came home, and that's when I told my parents everything. They had no idea what I had been through, and they blamed themselves. I told them that none of it was their fault.

I'd been having some medical problems around the time I came back, and the doctors didn't think that I was able to have children. So they gave me these pills. I went back after three months for some testing, and they were like, "Hey, guess what, you're pregnant." I didn't think I was going to have kids. They told me I couldn't have any. So, naturally, my whole lifestyle changed. I did everything by the book and just sort of pulled my life together. I had my daughter, Hannah, who's five now, got my GED, and went to college as soon as Hannah was old enough to go to day care.

When I came back to my reservation, it was like I was able to appreciate everything for the first time. I wanted Hannah to be raised around that and to know my family. So she's my little red-headed, blue-eyed daughter walking around telling everybody she's Blackfeet. She dances at the powwows and she knows a lot of Blackfeet words. It's kind of cute to see this little white baby walking around all the Indians.

There's a lot that I could teach Hannah about life and spirituality, but what she gets from my family and being around other people here already shows in the little things she does. She won't hurt a tree because she knows the tree has life; she has this great understanding of the spirit of things. She gets it. She won't hurt a grasshopper because he's alive and what if he has a family? It's just crazy what she grasps, and I know that's because we live there.

I don't ride much anymore. I rehabilitate horses if someone has abused them or if they've been injured. I work with them and help owners learn how to be their friend. Horses respond a lot quicker if you're accommodating to them. So I will work with and train horses, but I don't ride for pleasure. I'd rather take care of them—make sure they are healthy.

You can rehabilitate a horse that's been treated badly for years, but it's like working with a kid that's been abused—you have to take it slow, earn their trust and build their confidence, and then re-teach them from there.

Dr. Joseph McDonald

SALISH KOOTENAI
COFOUNDER AND PRESIDENT,
SALISH KOOTENAI COLLEGE
PABLO, MONTANA

WE HAVE A SIGN POSTED NEAR OUR CABIN ON FLATHEAD Lake, Montana, that reads "Glencoe." It's there to represent our Scottish heritage. Our clan comes from Glencoe in the Scotland Highlands. We were given the name because of an event that occurred during the English takeover of Scotland, when the clan chief refused to sign his allegiance to the king of England. The king decided to use our clan as an example to demonstrate to the other clans what would happen if they refused to sign as well. He ordered the killing of every man, woman, and child at Glencoe. Only about thirty were killed, and the rest escaped.

My great-great grandfather was Angus McDonald. My father's land, the land that I own now, is right at the trading post that Angus established, and so we were raised with stories about the Scottish fur trader. We were fascinated by how he took to the Indian people so easily, and how they took to him, and how he loved the outdoors and sleeping outside. In the summertime, family gathers at our cabin, and we have tents up everywhere and people sleep all over.

I've been to Scotland to see where Angus was born and where he traveled. There's a writer over there by the name of Jim Hunter who is a specialist in Highlands history and has done a considerable amount of research on Angus. Through him, I learned that Angus was one of the few Scottish fur traders that came over here and stayed. Most of them worked and then went back to Scotland.

When the McDonalds were taken over by the English, they lost their Gaelic language. They're trying to bring it back, though, and they have a little Gaelic college on the Island of Skye. Jim Hunter arranged for me to speak there. It was wonderful, because what we're trying to do here with the tribal colleges is very similar to what they're trying to do there with their college. I told them that my work as a college president isn't so different from the Indians' work in the early days. Back then, they hunted buffalo and gathered berries. I still hunt and gather—only I hunt and gather money for the college. By the end of the reception, unbeknownst to me, they had passed a hat around, and when I left, they gave me a big bag of money to bring home.

You wouldn't call these Scots indigenous, but in a way they are, because when you read the history of how they were treated by the English, it's not very different from the way Indians were treated by white people in the United States. The strange thing about that, though, is that after they got over here and had money and power, they became the oppressors.

I have four children, nine grandchildren, and one great-grandchild, and I've tried to teach them all about this part of their history, but I haven't taken them to Scotland yet. I'd like to, though, one of these years. One of my boys gave all his kids Scottish Highlander names—Katie, Annie, and Erin. It's my belief that you should be proud of every aspect of your heritage. Sometimes we get so caught up in the Indian movement that we kind of scorn our European heritage, and we shouldn't. We should be proud of it all, whether it's black or Asian or some despotic European tribe. We should be proud. And it's also important to have compassion for those people whose heritage includes Indian, because I think it gives them a sounder base for themselves.

I was raised in an Indian community, in an Indian family, and so those are my roots. That's the culture I practice, and while I don't have any intentions of ever wearing a kilt, I wouldn't mind learning to play the bagpipes.

Sheila M. Morris

OMAHA

ALUMNA, NEBRASKA INDIAN COMMUNITY COLLEGE
WALTHILL, NEBRASKA

I GUESS EVERYTHING IN MY LIFE IS IMPORTANT TO ME, BUT my degree is probably one of the most important things. I went back to school when I was thirty-eight years old. Oh, my God, I was so afraid. Thank God, it was a small college, because if I had to be around more than 500 people, I never would've made it.

My first day of college I wore one of my husband's shirts. It was an old dress shirt, and I wore polyester pants that were, like, from twenty years before, and white tennis shoes. To me, these were dress-up clothes. I didn't wear makeup. My hair was long and my husband didn't allow me to fix it or anything. I think the only reason that I stayed was because my younger sister went to school, and she pushed me into the classroom and made sure that I stayed there. But it was terrifying. My first class was math, and I almost walked out after about ten minutes because I had no idea what the teacher was talking about.

It was important for me to get a degree for myself, but it was more important to do it for my kids, because my circumstances at the time didn't allow me to do too much else for them. At that point in my life, I had no ambition. I lived the way my husband wanted me to live, and most of the time we weren't even together. He would come home for a couple of months and then go away, and I would be pregnant. Then he would come back again just before the baby was born and stay another couple of months. I really didn't realize the pattern. Every time he left I was pregnant again. A friend told me that I could make things better for my kids if I went back to school, and so, thanks to her, I went.

Probably for about five months during the coldest months, I hitchhiked to school because my car always broke down. Then, my husband destroyed my books. I just decided that I was going to keep going. I told my teachers that I didn't have any books and I didn't have any money, and so one of them made copies for me for the rest of the semester.

Up until that time, no one really knew what I had to go home to. When I was growing up, we didn't air our dirty laundry in public, and so a lot of times, after I'd been beaten, I wore glasses. I used a lot of makeup. I didn't put it on when I was at home. I waited until I got to the school, and then covered up whatever I could.

Sometimes I would have marks on my neck, and so I would wear scarves. I kept going because a part of me knew that if I was doing something my husband didn't want me to do, it had to be good for me. And, again, it was for my kids. I have seven kids.

It wasn't until after college that I understood what I was capable of. And the thing that I realized is that for the first ten years of my married life, I was a single parent. Even though my kids helped, it was me who kept the roof over our heads. It was just a surprise, because I kept thinking my husband did everything. When he came back for those three-month periods, it was like that's how I had to live. When I finally realized it was all me, I had the strength to walk out and say that's it.

I gave the speech at our graduation in 1995. In that speech, I told my classmates not to let anything stand in their way. That if you want something, the harder you have to fight for it the more important it will be to you. I talked about the importance of family and friends, because you need both to get through whatever it is. And that it's important for everyone to know that they're worth something—they can be whoever they want to be, regardless of skin color. It doesn't matter where you come from, it's what's inside you. I guess that's the most important thing for people to know. It was a nightmare for me in the beginning, but I lived through it and I survived and it gets better. Every day it gets better.

Wade I. Teeple

BAY MILLS INDIAN COMMUNIITY

OFF-CAMPUS COORDINATOR/
CONTRACTS-GRANTS OFFICER,
BAY MILLS COMMUNITY COLLEGE
BRIMLEY, MICHIGAN

WHEN I'M NOT WORKING, ME AND MY WIFE, SHARON LEE, we have a boat, and if the weather's nice, I like to get out and just do some hook-and-line fishing, perch or whatever. It's a 19-foot boat, and we got a port-a-potty on there, too, and so we take a lunch with us and just go. Sharon Lee and I hardly talk when we're out there. Just a little bit when I've got the radio on and she tells me to turn it off. Out there in that little bay—it's just a drop in the bucket compared to Whitefish Bay thirty miles straight across. I've been on some big seas out there.

I grew up almost directly across the road from the college, back when there was nothing here. We didn't have streetlights. Roads were paved in the 1950s, but they were kind of rounded roads, and in the wintertime, you had to watch what you were doing or you'd be in a ditch. There was no employment other than commercial fishing, which is a hard way to make a living. A lot of people left to go to the city to try to get jobs in the automotive factories. But since we built the first Native American casino up here in Bay Mills in July of 1984, we've had quite an influx of people coming back.

I used to be the chief of police here on this reservation in the late 1970s, and things just weren't going right. We didn't get along with the Bay Mills tribal government, and they didn't like the way we were doing things as police officers. Finally, I said, "Well, you know, one way to make a change here is to run for tribal chair." So, I did and I won. I learned a lot from being a police officer, though. I learned that you've got to keep your head all the time, and that you can't fly off the handle or let something bother you too much because you never know what's going to happen. You've got to be in control of the situation. And that helped me. I was the president and tribal chair at Bay Mills for seven or eight years.

I believe that with everything you do, you should be able to stand behind it. You've got to live with yourself. In the tribal government, everything I did as president and chair was on the up and up, because—and the same went for when I was a police officer—if you're going to enforce the law, you first have to obey it.

I traveled to a lot of different states when I was in the military, back before I moved here to live permanently. I also got around quite a bit from being involved with the tribal government, but

I never found nothing as right as here in the Upper Peninsula of Michigan. You watch the news about the flooding that's going on over in the Minnesota area, the Red River, earthquakes, and tornadoes—we don't get that up here. We may have to put up with the cold weather from probably November to the end of March or early April, but our house is going to be here tomorrow. I just can't find any other place that I would rather be.

You have to lead by example. There's freedom in that. I went to jump school when I first started in the military and I'll tell you, once your chute opens, it's quite a feeling. You come out of this loud, roaring airplane, and at night, even when there are those tiny lights along the bottom of the jump seat, if the moon isn't out, it's like jumping into a black void. When you get down close enough, you try to see the tops of the trees so that you can prepare to land.

Sometimes, when you first come out, you spin around and you can't get your head up to see if your chute is open. The trainer tells you to look at the guys beside you: if you can see them, and you're falling at the same speed as they are and their chutes are open, then your chute is open. But if you can't see them, then you just have to try to kick and make sure you get that canopy open. And then it's like you're floating. I mean, just free. It's what you came for.

Les Northrup Sr.

**FOND DU LAC BAND
OF LAKE SUPERIOR CHIPPEWA**
CHIEF SECURITY OFFICER, RECRUITER, AND ALUMNUS,
FOND DU LAC TRIBAL AND COMMUNITY COLLEGE
CLOQUET, MINNESOTA

THE IMPORTANCE OF EDUCATION WAS ALWAYS STRESSED upon me by my parents, by some of the elders in the community, and also by my grandfather and grandmother on my mother's side. My grandma used to say, "You need more than a high school diploma to provide for your family."

I have four children and my wife has four children and we have two children together. Out of the ten kids, every one of them graduated from high school and, well, let's see, we've got three that earned an undergraduate degree. My youngest one has an associate's degree from Fond du Lac Tribal and Community College, and I graduated with her from the law enforcement program: she got an associate of science degree in business and I had the associate of arts in law enforcement. We walked across the stage together to receive our diplomas.

When I finished the law enforcement program, Fond du Lac named an award after me because I was able to do everything the younger students did. I didn't do as much as the athletic kids, but I stuck right in there. The plaque reads: "Fond du Lac Tribal and Community College Law Enforcement and Skills Program for the New Millennium: Les Northrup Award presented to Les Northrup, a respected elder and fellow classmate, for his wisdom, vision, and leadership in his ongoing quest to improve himself and his community." They'll be giving it out every year from now on.

I also have a degree from the University of Minnesota. I graduated in 1979 with a bachelor's of fine arts in teaching history, and I got a bachelor's of fine science in Indian studies, so I've taken advantage of the educational system.

Right now I'm working with Fond du Lac on sort of a month-to-month basis. I did recruiting for them this summer at the reservations and tribal schools and community centers, trying to get new recruits into the law enforcement and corrections program and any other programs that we have. I also signed on to set up security on campus. The college is currently doing a lot of expansion—two more dormitories, a little more parking space—so there's going to be need for security. Nothing has happened yet, but you never want to be caught short.

I recruited at about eight powwows and must've gotten about a hundred interested students. Probably ninety were Indian students, and about ten were non-Indian. I had a ten-by-ten-foot tent and inside I had a table with different information about the school. I had a Fond du Lac Tribal and Community College banner, and then I put some of the law enforcement badges on just to draw attention. A lot of people don't ask you what you're doing, but when you start talking to them, they get more interested.

Three of my daughters and a couple of my grandkids were there with me, too. The youngest grandson plays the drums. It was nice recruiting and hearing the drumbeat at the same time. It was just like going to a movie and listening to the music. I had a chance to dance some of the ceremonial dances, too. I'm not a veteran, but my dad and my uncles were, and I always dance to honor them.

Law enforcement is about respect for the law. And that's what I tell young people when I'm recruiting: Don't break the law. If you want to get into a law enforcement program, you can't beat up a woman or a man or fight and hurt and rob people. You can't do that.

Being semiretired is kind of a nice place to be at, but there are always things I have to do. I have to get some firewood ready for the winter. I cut the grass occasionally. I did a little garden work this summer. I fix up things and spend time with the grandkids, pick them up at school.

I gave the college commencement address this year. I talked about the school and the importance of ethnic diversity and self-worth, ethics, and leadership. I told the students that they are all leaders and that they should never compromise their ethics for any amount of money. Then I told them about how I used to think that there was just the red man and the white man. But now I know we have the yellow man, the black man, a lot of cultural diversity, and that they need to learn about that. If you live in a multicultural society, you must learn to get along with other people.

Dr. Guy Gorman Sr.

NAVAJO
COFOUNDER, DINÉ COLLEGE
(FKA NAVAJO COMMUNITY COLLEGE)
CHINLE, ARIZONA

MY WIFE, JUANITA, AND I, WE PARTICIPATE IN WHAT THEY call song and dance. It's not a religious thing, but it's kind of similar to dances performed at religious ceremonies. We sing and we dance, and our house is full of trophies and plaques for what we have done with that. I wish I could count how many we got, but it's too many.

I did not get a college education. I took some college courses, but never got any kind of degree. Only thing I got is an honorary degree from Diné College. All my life I have concerns about the Navajo kids and their schools. They need to learn a lot so we can live like the rest of the people in the United States—in New York or Chicago or places like that. For me, that is one of the things that I kept thinking about throughout my life: How can we prepare kids and how can we do this quickly? I used to preach stuff like this. Now, it's kind of getting lost. I was on the Navajo Tribal Council for twenty years, but I'm no longer on that. I'm retired now.

Three of us kind of started this whole thing, the idea about building a college. This was when I was serving on the education committee of the tribal council. The Bureau of Indian Affairs (BIA) had total control of all the education on the Navajo Nation. Well, they wouldn't even let you go into the school where your kids were learning. This was a really terrible thing that was going on and we didn't like it. We kept after the BIA. It was two other people and me, they're both gone now, and then we decided to take over the school. We wanted to start something that would represent the way all education should be run as far as the Navajo are concerned. It was the beginning of something bigger.

When they put me in school, I didn't know a word of English. All I knew was Navajo. Now I'm eighty years old; I speak English, I've been married fifty years, I've traveled all over, been in the service, and I've got five grown sons. All my sons are men now. They all went to college and have good jobs. The oldest one, he's a construction inspector, and then the next one, he's a computer man. And then the third one, he works with computers, too, and he's working with the tribe now in Window Rock. He's also a silversmith. He made the bolo I'm wearing here. He takes photographs and makes an image and then engraves it. He's pretty famous. It's really expensive jewelry. Then the fourth one, he's living here and working with the community's Public Health Services. And the last one, he and his wife are teachers in the Chinle Public Schools.

We've got a granddaughter that just went back to Phillips Exeter Academy in New Hampshire. That's a private high school with students from all over the world. That's where she's going to school. She's pretty smart and has all kinds of ideas. And I got five other grandchildren. Two boys are in Atlanta, Georgia—they're roller skate racers. A couple of weeks ago one of them almost made the world championship. He and his brother travel all over the United States for competitions.

It's important that my grandchildren know their history and live and remember the Navajo way of life. They understand when I talk to them about it, and my granddaughter at Exeter speaks Navajo. She's not shy about that. Two of my elder in-laws are Anglos, and so that's a different factor, but we kind of understand and try to get along the best way we can.

Tracey Jilot

CHIPPEWA-CREE

HEAD LIBRARIAN, STONE CHILD COLLEGE
ROCKY BOY, MONTANA

MY AUNT PEGGY NAGEL WAS PRESIDENT OF STONE CHILD College, where I now work as the librarian. She was a huge influence in my life and in helping me to become who I am.

I barely graduated from high school. I had no interest whatsoever in going to college. I fought going for eight years and came up with every possible excuse to avoid college. Then I got it in my mind that I wanted to become a Lutheran minister, but found out that the only way I could do that was by attending a four-year university or college. So I knew it had to be done, but I was deathly afraid. I just never thought that I could be educated. I never had the confidence in myself to believe that I could do it.

I was accepted into Stone Child College, but I was also a firefighter at the time. Two weeks before school started, I went out on a twenty-one-day fire. When I came back, I was two weeks behind. By the time Peggy was finished with me, I was enrolled in classes. She told me that she would do everything in her power to help me catch up and get through, which she did. It was crazy because the building where she had her office happened also to be where the student services were, and so I couldn't avoid her. She would come out of her office or call me in, just to see what I was doing and to give me encouragement. One day at the end of the semester, I happened to look up on the board where student grade-point averages were posted, and I swear I never thought it was possible, but I looked up on that board and saw that I had a 4.0.

I was so excited, I ran all over the place with a big old smile on my face. Peggy called me into her office and said, "So, I see your name is up on my board and you've got a 4.0." I told her how grateful I was to her. She said that I was the one who did all the studying, all the work, and that I'm the one who got the 4.0. From then on, that was it.

When I got out of school, I needed to make a decision about what to do with my life. Peggy sat me down and asked me what my plans were. When I told her that I was unsure, she asked if I'd consider working at Stone Child. So, that's what I ended up doing, and I've been here ever since.

Peggy always had us all working on one common mission: to do everything in our power to help students continue on with their education, and to help them do well and to enjoy it. And I've never seen more people work harder at achieving a common goal under an individual's leadership than I did at Stone Child when Peggy was alive.

I remember the exact time I heard. It was ten o'clock in the evening, and I was at home. My friend called and told me she had just heard that Peggy had passed away. We were just lost. According to the minister at the funeral service, Peggy and her husband were in their house when they both started to feel dizzy. It was a carbon monoxide leak. Peggy's husband had tried to get them both out, but Peggy knew she wasn't going to make it and that if he kept trying to get her out, too, then neither of them would make it. She made him get out to save himself, and that doesn't surprise me in any way, because that's just the way Peggy was.

For Peggy, working at Stone Child College was and is a way to give back to our reservation and to try to get us into a better mindset about what we need for our future. Before Stone Child ever came into existence, the number of Native individuals getting a bachelor's degree was very low. And if you did leave the reservation to get an education, people assumed you were trying to be better than everybody else. During the initial stages of setting up a college here, a lot was talked about on taking the negative connotation out of education. To say, "Yes, you can go get your degree and then come back and help your reservation." That's what Peggy was about.

Vine Deloria Jr.

AUTHOR AND HISTORIAN
STANDING ROCK SIOUX
GOLDEN, COLORADO

I DON'T CONSIDER WHAT I DO AS WORK—READING, researching, and writing is fun. If pressed to say what it is that I do when I am technically not working, I guess I like to watch old movies, gossip and email with friends, and spend lots of time in bookstores.

I remember when I decided to become a writer. It was the late 1960s—the height of the Civil Rights Movement and the beginning of the American Indian Movement. For that reason, at that time, publishing houses and editors felt that the next big trend in marketable books would be Indians. Once when I was planning a trip to New York City for business as a political activist, Macmillan Publishing Company somehow found out that I was coming and invited me to meet with an editor over lunch. I thought, Why not? It's a free lunch.

At the meeting, the editor asked if I would be willing to write a book. Although I had no experience or background as a writer, I was an Indian, and he felt that was enough. He handed me a check for five hundred dollars as an advance, and I left the meeting with no idea what I would write about. More important, I had enough money in my pocket to live off while I was in law school.

It wasn't until after my first year of law school when I actually realized that I had signed a contract with a publisher, but had yet to begin any work on the book. After much thought, I decided I would write about the Bureau of Indian Affairs and government relations from a Native perspective. I wanted non-Native people to understand the ongoing malfeasance of the United States government in its relationship with American Indian Nations. I wanted to humanize Indians, to go beyond the stoic stereotypes prevalent in U.S. culture, and to allow others to understand our perspective.

I finished a few chapters and sent them to my editor in New York. When I arrived at the Macmillan building to meet and talk about the pages, I felt certain that my editor would find my writing too frank, too radical, and too angry for mass appeal or marketability. As I approached his office, I decided that rather than opening the door, through which he would most surely throw my chapters at me, I would stand behind the glass panel to the right of the door. With surprise, I watched as he saw me, jumped out from behind his

desk, and gestured me to come in, gushing over my phenomenal writing, asking excitedly when I would have more chapters completed. I was dumbfounded. He gave me another check for five hundred dollars, and I left, returning home to quickly finish the rest of the book.

I must say, my editor was very cunning and clever. A month before the book was to be published, in 1969, he met with several well-known book critics. *Custer Died for Your Sins: An American Indian Manifesto* was printed with the critics' glowing comments on the cover and promptly sold out its first and second runs.

I did finish law school, but didn't want to practice law. Writing, though, I wanted to do. I had found a way to develop issues in a wide variety of areas, to identify a pattern and gather data to see if it has any substance, and to discover things that have been missed by others. Writing was, and still is, the best tool I can think of when it comes to challenging the norm.

Dr. Janine Pease-Pretty On Top

CROW

FORMER PRESIDENT,
LITTLE BIG HORN COLLEGE
LODGE GRASS, MONTANA

MY NAME IN THE CROW LANGUAGE MEANS "ONE WHO loves to pray." I was named by Lizzie Yellowtail, who told my parents that the reason she had lived such a long, wonderful, and blessed life is because she loved to pray and prayed often. Lizzie Yellowtail was the mother of Robert Yellowtail, one of the Crow Tribe's most famous leaders, and she lived to be 108.

This photograph is taken in the common grounds in the Lodge Grass District, where my family has been for probably six generations. I'm a member of the Valley of the Chiefs District in the Crow Tribe, and this particular place is where we were once located after the last secessions of land. Our reservation started out as 38 million acres, and it's now down to 2.1 million acres. Lodge Grass District is where our band, Mountain Crow, is primarily located, and it's a beautiful valley, and so it is called the Valley of the Chiefs.

This is where we have all of our social events, political rallies, and a lot of family events. In the earliest days, quite a number of our district members had their homes here, and now it's a place where we hold social gatherings. We have dances in the summertime, and in the wintertime we have games, and then horse riding events in the spring. It's a very important common ground. It's also where we pick chokecherries during the season.

The chokecherry bush is very hardy and can withstand the 40-below weather that we have here in Montana. The cherries start to flourish and ripen at the end of July, and they're ready to pick through September. I probably canned my first crop on my own around 1970, when I first had my own kitchen and started canning cherries for our family ceremonies. When Crow babies first walk or talk, we have fry bread and chokecherry pudding, and so when my babies were little, I had my relatives over and got out the cherries.

There are several parts to our traditional meal. We have fruit, which would certainly be chokecherries, June berries, lots of different berries that I pick or make into pudding. Some people might buy canned fruit from a store nowadays. Then we have meat, which would probably be buffalo, elk, deer, venison, or, of course, beef. Then we have corn, zucchini, or some sort of a vegetable.

Not only do we gather fruit, but my son hunts and we dry all different kinds of meat. Turnips, onions, carrots, and things grow on the land everywhere, which we dry and keep for our stews and other various foods that we make in the winter. There's a low-lying bush in the woods that we use to make tea. It tastes like wood smells. We gather peppermint and raspberry. There are eight or ten different kinds of tea that I gather in the winter: some of it for medicine and some of it is just to go with a meal. My kids have grown up knowing all of this, and now my grandchildren are learning. We live in a rich, beautiful countryside, and we have to know where things grow, where they can be harvested, and how they are cared for.

I recently turned fifty-three years old, and Ms. Pease-Pretty On Top is no longer married. I'm a single mom and a single grand-mom. I have two children: Roses Holds is twenty-seven and Vernon Windy Boy is twenty-three; and two grandchildren: Tillie Stewart is four and Kayden Joel is two. I've always emphasized to them how important it is that we have managed to earn a living on the northern plains of Montana.

The other day, Tillie, who's in the picture with me, said, "I picked some of those cherries, didn't I?" Gathering and harvesting is something that our whole family has done together for many years. I can remember going on cherry-picking picnics, and when the whole crop was in, my auntie or my mom would can, dry, or freeze them. It was a big event, and it's still that way. Now I'm the elder lady and my little grandkids are the little helpers.

Dr. David M. Gipp

STANDING ROCK SIOUX, HUNKPAPA LAKOTA

PRESIDENT, UNITED TRIBES
TECHNICAL COLLEGE
BISMARCK, NORTH DAKOTA

I HAVE A COUPLE OF CROSS-COUNTRY BIKES AND ONE RACER, but I don't use that one very much. I ride at my leisure, just to clear my mind. It's a good way to get away from it all. I ride anywhere from 20 to 50 miles or so. That's not much on a bike, really. I used to be into running, but not much anymore, mostly because of shin splints from years ago. Biking and some walking are what I do to stay healthy.

One of the things we've been working on here at the United Tribes Technical College (UTTC) is the health and wellness initiative, which started about three weeks ago. We've decided to build a physical wellness center as part of the overall program to help change attitudes about general well-being, because as much as you need to be physically healthy, you also need to understand nutritional and attitudinal aspects of wellness.

I don't know if I'm the best at leading by example, but I'm trying. I won't win the physical fitness contest, but I don't know that I rank at the bottom either. I do bike on campus, and I think it's important for students to see more of us doing those kinds of things, or just taking a walk around the school, promoting and participating in physical activity.

I've been associated with UTTC since the beginning. I worked as a sort of tribal planner with the corporate division of the United Tribes from 1969 to 1972. I was acting executive director for about four or five months during that time, and then eventually we started AIHEC—American Indian Higher Education Consortium—in 1973, and I started here as president in 1977. I had my official twenty-fifth anniversary on May 2, 2002. Later in the year, in September, we had a big honoring and give-away ceremony during the International Powwow, which is the Indian way for most of the tribes. They held a special ceremony and made a number of presentations to me. I'd say we probably had a record turnout. Lots of dancers from everywhere. Thirty-six drums, I think they had. So it was a special, very moving gathering.

I think we've succeeded at making some solid improvements at UTTC over the past twenty-five years. We've moved from being nonaccredited to being fully accredited through the year 2011. We got the full ten-year accreditation without stipulation last year, in 2001, when we were evaluated by the North Central Association of Colleges and Schools. We still have to demonstrate that we're making progress, of course, but we're also able to look at new programs and make plans for expansion. We've acquired 135 additional acres to the south of us, so we're planning to add a whole new campus that will serve over 2,000 students in addition to our current 400-plus.

There's always more to work on. There are so many young Indian people that are in need of better education and more opportunities. The tribal colleges can provide that. I see young people come here from other populations or from our own communities, and they seem to be getting younger and younger. Of course, I'm getting older. But I really just see that these young people want more for themselves and their families and want to learn how they can improve their lives. It's pretty inspiring.

It's a whole new and different generation. I actually think that they face more difficult barriers than we ever did. Some of it has to do with the classroom and learning adequately at the primary and secondary levels of education, and some of it deals with social and environmental conditions—maybe we didn't have to put up with as much. For instance, certainly alcohol was an issue for my generation, and I'm not saying that it was good, but now I see young people concerned with the abuse of alcohol and drugs in a way that we never were. And gangs are far more prevalent than when I was growing up, both in urban and rural settings. So we really need to work in our tribal colleges at helping our youth re-identify with who they are, what their tribe is about, and even what some of their roles and responsibilities are.

That's why I always enjoy the powwows, because I see the little ones dancing out there. They are dancing away already, and in that moment they are learning while they are watching their peers, older brothers and sisters, their mothers and fathers, and grandparents.

Jarett D. Medicine Elk

**NORTHERN CHEYENNE
AND ASSINIBOINE**
MISSIONARY, CHURCH OF LATTER-DAY SAINTS,
AND ALUMNUS, FORT PECK COMMUNITY COLLEGE
ELK CITY, OKLAHOMA

THIS IS HOW WE DRESS ALL THE TIME. MY GRANDFATHER was the first to convert. He was of a different faith for a long time before meeting some missionaries on the reservation. They talked with him and told him about the Mormon faith. He listened to what they had to say, but he wanted to observe them before he was willing to commit. After a while, he finally converted. Then my mother was born into it, and so was I.

For me, it's like any religion you're born into—you have to decide for yourself whether or not it's right for you, something that you like and want to be involved in. I had always heard stories from my parents, grandparents, and older people in our community about the missionaries and how they would come to help others. There's a Mormon hymn that I really like, and part of it says: "In the quiet heart is hidden Sorrow that the eye can't see." And it goes on: "I would be my brother's keeper; I would learn the healer's art." What that means is that there is always more to somebody, more to their heart, than can be seen. That person needs help with the trials that he or she is going through, and that's where the missionaries come in.

I'm currently on my first church-sent mission. It's in Oklahoma. I'd never been here before. People say it's the buckle of the Bible Belt. In Utah, you see a Latter-day Saints church on every block. But here in Oklahoma, you see a different faith church on every block. There are, of course, a lot of Oklahoma football fans down here, and I hope I get to serve on a college campus at some point during my mission. But Oklahoma hasn't won me over yet. It's been really hot, and we're walking around with our shirts and ties. A lot of time people let us in the door just because they feel sorry for us and want to give us water.

I'll be here for two years, and I've been here a little over seven months. Two of my cousins had been on missions before, and I asked them what it was like. All they could tell me was that it was the best time in their lives. They couldn't really explain it beyond that because it's just one of those things that you have to experience yourself. Since I've been here, I would definitely say I've had the best time, and I will probably always look back on it as the foundation for my life.

We work with families and individuals, and what's interesting is that even though I may not actually be a part of that family, I have insight into what's going on. That's what allows me to help them in the ways they need, which, in turn, helps me to gain understanding of myself.

I went to school in Idaho for two years on what's called the Placement Program. It was designed by the church for kids from the reservation to live with a Mormon family during the school year. The program was founded when my mother went to school, and so I'd heard a lot about it. The experience helped to prepare me for my mission, in terms of being away from my family. I am allowed to call them twice a year, but other than that, we correspond through e-mail and letters. Actually, one of the students who I went to school with in Idaho is serving a mission in Oklahoma now, too. So that's been nice to run into someone familiar, but that's not uncommon with the Latter-day Saints. It's like Indian Country, where there's maybe two degrees of separation. You always have a family no matter where you go.

We get no salary or hourly wage. We have to save money to go on a mission, and I worked a lot before I started. My family helped me out, and friends in the community will help if I should come up short at any time. So there is the assurance that I will always have enough money to finish my mission. There have been many missionaries, though, who have started out with very little money and no additional support. We estimate that it costs about $10,000 to sustain yourself on a two-year mission.

A lot of the money I saved came from my internship at Allstate Insurance Company outside of Chicago through a program coordinated by the American Indian College Fund. One of the greatest lessons that I learned at Allstate was diversity. There are people out there from many different races and backgrounds. You can learn so much from those people, and you come to realize that you or your people were not the only ones who suffered hardship throughout history.

Every person develops their own cultural comfort zone. And life is about learning to leave that security. You may know what situations will arise in your comfort zone, but once you're away from it, you don't really know anything.

Dr. Gerald "Carty" Monette

TURTLE MOUNTAIN BAND OF CHIPPEWA
PRESIDENT, TURTLE MOUNTAIN
COMMUNITY COLLEGE
BELCOURT, NORTH DAKOTA

I'M PRESIDENT OF THE TURTLE MOUNTAIN COMMUNITY College. That's what I do, all day long, almost every day of the week. This is it. I live on a lake and I have a boat. Sometimes I stay home and fish with the kids. On special occasions, I let my hair down. And I have a hoop. I mean, I shoot baskets. I'm a pretty good shot. But I haven't had my glasses off much since I was eight years old, and I'm fairly defined by my work.

I didn't know exactly how it would happen, but I always knew that I wanted to contribute to the reservation community. Back when I was coming up, education was the way to do it. Turtle Mountain is one of the first tribal colleges—we're one of the original six—and this year marks our thirtieth anniversary. Our institution had a very humble beginning. We still try as hard today as we did when we started to attain our goals and to fulfill our mission statement. We're by no means there, and on a scale of 1 to 10, we're probably at 3 or 4, because there's always so much more that can be done to build this institution to serve our community.

I came on board officially with Turtle Mountain in May of 1974—unofficially, I was involved before then, attending meetings while I was still in graduate school during 1973. It was originally called the Turtle Mountain Enrichment Center, but everybody was thinking tribal college and not enrichment center. The name changed in 1977-78 when it became an accredited college.

I didn't start out as the president. In my first year of employment with Turtle Mountain, I was a codirector, but I changed that, because I didn't think codirectors could function effectively. I suggested that we have a director and an assistant director. The director would be housed at the state campus forty miles from here, and the assistant director would reside here on the reservation—that's the position I took.

I was in charge of internal functions on the reservation and the director of external functions. That director, Larry Belgarde, then became the first president of Turtle Mountain Community College when we found enough money to hire a president. Later, I became the director, and the assistant director position was removed. A few years after that—maybe 1977—Larry left the institution, and I became president of the college. I've been here ever since.

The majority of tribal members still don't understand the value of higher education—a whole bunch of them do, but the majority of them do not. That's not the case in other communities because in America, whether you go to college or don't go to college, there's an inherent value placed on higher education. We're only just starting to learn the process of putting that into play.

I think the biggest challenge I've encountered as president of Turtle Mountain Community College, and also as a member of the Native community, has been making the transition to where we are today. The way our people experience change is what causes our issues with housing and unemployment and education and transportation, and, so, that's the biggest challenge. Many tribal members have difficulty with that adjustment.

Indian people want very much to retain their tribal languages and cultures, and that creates a tension. As we're trying to adapt to the changing world, we're also trying to adjust to having the right to retain our culture and our history. For a long time, the policy of the government was to get rid of Indian cultures and languages. Then they decided it was okay, but subsequently, we've had a hard time accepting that privilege—the power to retain what is ours, and figuring out where that fits in with the way we live.

Alphonso Colegrove

HOOPA VALLEY AND YUROK
ALUMNUS, NORTHWEST INDIAN COLLEGE
BELLINGHAM, WASHINGTON

THIS HAT IS REALLY CLOSE TO MY HEART. WHEN I WAS A youngster, for birthdays or for Christmas, my brothers and sisters and I would all get matching hats from my mom. But over the years, my mom's had two kidney transplants, and she has a lot of problems with arthritis. So the hats have been a lot fewer and far between. This hat is actually the last one I got from her. It was kind of a special order, because I had gotten a tattoo on my arm, which is of flying geese, and I asked her to make me a hat with the same design and colors, maroon and black. So the tattoo and my hat match. It's a Hoopa design, but my mom is Yurok.

My mom is a very traditional Yurok woman—very quiet, but very strong. She raised nine kids and is putting up with numerous grandchildren and great-grandchildren. Because she's had two kidney transplants, she goes to dialysis three times a week. I know it's very trying and very hard for her, but she's doing it.

What gets me by at home on the reservation is the fact that I know all the dances, so no one gives me a hard time about not knowing the language. There are some dances that are specific to our area and that happen every summer; one is the Brush Dance. Two others that happen every two or four years are the White Deer Skin Dance and the Jump Dance. We do the Brush Dance in about nine different places—two places for the Hoopa Valley Tribe, two for the Yurok Tribe, and a few for the Karuk Tribe. We'll dance on a Thursday night, maybe twice, and then Saturday we'll dance all night. The dance is meant to help heal a baby or to prevent any sickness from coming to that baby. In the dance pit, we usually dance around a mother and a child. It's a chance for people of the different tribes to come together and share their culture, to help support each other and show unity.

Dancing is especially important to me, because my family is both Hoopa and Yurok, and I participate for both. And it's a way to honor my mother and my father, who I lost to cancer a few years ago. He was my role model. That's how I took the direction that I first chose—to be a logger and a firefighter—because that's what he did. He raised us boys to be hunters and fishermen, but he really wanted me to do something else with my life, too. I spent the last month and a half of his life with him, and after we lost him, I decided to go to school.

I knew there were better opportunities for me. And, unfortunately, I knew I wasn't going to be able to find them on my reservation. I had to go away to get an education so that I could provide a better future for myself. Not only that, I wanted to be a role model for other people back on the reservation. So in the summer of 1999, me and my girlfriend, who is now my wife, were looking for a school, and she came across Northwest Indian College on the Internet. To tell the truth, because where I grew up in Northern California was so isolated, I didn't even know that there were any tribal colleges out there. We were both accepted, caught the train the day after Christmas, and we've been there ever since.

The tribal college has been great for me. Ever since I enrolled, things have just taken off. I'm majoring in computers, and I can actually see a better and brighter future for myself. I can imagine more than just going back to the reservation, and I can envision myself working in a corporate environment, or owning and operating my own business. When you go to a tribal college, you don't feel like a minority like you would at a more traditional college. You are the majority, so you can be at peace, feel at home, and be yourself. Since I've been at Northwest Indian College, I've also met a lot of tribal college students who I know are going places and who could benefit from knowing someone who owned and operated his own business. I plan to provide that opportunity.

Gerald One Feather

OGLALA LAKOTA
COFOUNDER, OGLALA LAKOTA COLLEGE
OGLALA, SOUTH DAKOTA

I'VE DONE POLICE WORK AND I'VE DONE POLITICS AND I'VE done academia and I've taught ever since 1973. I teach the foundation of values and the original concept of tiospaye, which is a Lakota word for "extended family." I've been trying to retire for the last year, to get out, but the more I try to step out of work, the more I'm involved. I'm chairman of the Elders Council at the Oglala Lakota College in Kyle, South Dakota—there is one from each district who serves as adviser to the president of the college.

Yesterday I went to the school for a meeting, and we approved a linguistics institute so we're going to have a language program at the college, and then here they come and told me I'm appointed to the board of trustees. So it's just one thing after another. This is the first time they're going to put an elder on the board of trustees.

I'm one of the founders of the college, and back then we promoted the GED a lot. That was the main point of the college. The second goal was preserving Lakota language and culture. The third thing was certification for whatever career a student wanted to pursue. Any job they seek, there'll be certification in the end, like teaching or nursing or social work or engineering. So those are three elements that started the college. It was tough because we tangled with the South Dakota Board of Regents. They were against it. They said, "There are too many colleges. Why try to create another one?" The governor was opposed to it and the president of the University of South Dakota got fired for trying to help us. So basically I went down to Colorado and got the president of the University of Colorado involved. At the time, he was the chairman of the Academy of Science at the White House. And with his help, the college got accepted into the system.

We have a decentralized campus and nine centers that are based on the needs of the area. Whatever the area's needs, they are met through the college, and each center has an advisory board, but the board of trustees at the main campus maintains the overall policy. Each center is different. They named a center after me. I'm the only one alive that's got a center named after him. All the other eight centers are named after dead people, but one's alive.

I'm diabetic, and I was in a coma three years ago for ten days. There was a 50/50 chance, I guess, of coming out alive. That was the closest to death I came. I'm all right now. I go on my own vision quests, ten times in my life, you know, and I stay out there four days at a time, so I know what I'm talking about.

Margarett Campbell

FORT PECK ASSINIBOINE

VICE PRESIDENT, COMMUNITY SERVICES,
FORT PECK COMMUNITY COLLEGE
POPLAR, MONTANA

I BELIEVE THAT IN ORDER TO PROVIDE STRONG AND SUSTAIN-able leadership, a leader must be personally well grounded, and that comes through an appreciation for the basic elements in life. For me, those elements are my belief in a higher power, my love of horses and the sport of rodeo, and the time I spend with my grandchildren.

My family has been involved in Indian rodeo for years, and during the 1960s, participated in the Professional Rodeo Cowboys Association. An important part of raising my own children was teaching them to honor and enjoy the unique relationship between a child and a horse—a dynamic that can ultimately help a child grow into a strong adult and a capable leader. A leader's success is measured by the guidance he or she provides within a community. A community is made up of families, so families need to be unified by whatever means possible: through powwowing, sacred religion, gardening, farming, or rodeo.

I lost my son in 1999, and a very significant part of my healing process was spending time with my horses. When things were the roughest, I would go out to the corral and my horse would be standing there, his head hanging—he could sense my grief and actually changed his manner toward me. A relationship like that is so important to establish. It's really very simple, and it costs nothing. The healing power of the exchanges between a horse and a person is not new information: there have been movies made and books written about it. But I will say that I now see families doing things together through horsemanship. I haven't always seen that.

I barrel-raced and roped as a teenager, but I'm not the famous one. My dad, Michael "Buddy" Campbell, was a PRCA cowboy, and I have two brothers who were in rodeo, too. My oldest daughter made her way through college on a rodeo scholarship and qualified for the National and State High School Rodeos, as well as the Indian National Rodeo. She's now a well-known cowgirl living in Albuquerque. And my two youngest daughters, and my son before he passed away, won a number of trophy saddles and buckles. So, horses and rodeo have really been an integral part of our family culture.

I have three grandchildren, soon to have four, and there's just something about having a grandchild that is so different from having your own child. It's such a special relationship that I've often had trouble articulating what it means to me. It completely changed the quality of my life. As a mother, I was so concerned with making sure that my children's bedrooms were clean and that their hair was parted straight, that their pants were ironed and their books were placed just so in their bookcases that I wasn't able to really relax and enjoy them as much as I do my grandchildren. With my grandchildren, I can be in the middle of preparing a big dinner, and if one of them comes and wants to play with me, I just turn the burners off and go roll around with them on the carpet. That's how we spend our time together. As a mother, that would not have happened because I was too worried about keeping things in order and running the household.

Grandparents play an essential role in passing on the oral history and knowledge base of our culture as Indians. Children may hear stories over and over again, but until we tell our history in a certain way, they won't retain its significance. Only as you get older do you start to recognize the value of certain information. I'm sorry that I didn't pay more attention to the stories my dad told me when I was a child, but I always assumed he would be there for me to ask. It's hard, because so many of our elders have passed on. Much of our history is oral, so we're left to try and piece together what we can. But I'm willing to take the time to do that.

In this society, we don't have any control over how rapidly things progress in technology. The one thing that we can control is our personal lives. We can say, "I'm going to remove myself from this stressful situation and deal with the basic elements of feeling secure, comfortable, and loved."

Richard B. Williams

OGLALA LAKOTA
EXECUTIVE DIRECTOR,
AMERICAN INDIAN COLLEGE FUND
DENVER, COLORADO

*— a Good Way
Rip o lu*

MY PASSION FOR CARS PROBABLY COMES FROM GROWING up in a home where there were no cars. We had to walk everywhere. It wasn't until 1969, when I got out of high school, that I actually had my first automobile—a 1955 Ford. Nothing fancy, just a plain old Ford. It had a value of about fifty dollars. My brother-in-law gave it to me when he went into the service and was sent off to Vietnam. He thought he was never coming back, so he gave me his car. He did come back, but I kept the car.

The ability to fix cars grew out of a necessity to have the car repaired. When you're poor and you don't have any money, you can't afford to take your car to a mechanic. You have to learn how to fix it yourself. And so I became a self-taught, shade-tree mechanic. There were many years when my wife would make fun of me because all I read were auto repair manuals. It wasn't until I went to graduate school that I developed a passion for reading stuff beyond auto repair manuals.

Over the years, as I've developed more financial resources for myself, I've still done auto work, not because I have to do it, but because I want to do it. It has become a very therapeutic thing for me to be able to go out into the garage and work on improvements rather than repairs. It's not that if I don't get it done, I can't go to the store or I can't go to work. It's just relaxing, and it's also gratifying, because unlike a lot of other things you might do, there's a real beginning and an end to it. I mean, if you change the brakes on the car, then you get in that car and the brakes work.

In my business at the College Fund, I don't ever see the direct results of a project after it begins. For example, when you give a student a scholarship, the scholarship itself is not the result. It's a long, drawn-out process that begins with a meeting in which you ask somebody for money, and goes on in order to maintain that funding. At the end of the day, I can't specifically state that I have helped fifty students. Whereas, if I'm working on a car, I can resolutely state that I have fixed the water pump. I repaired the radiator. I painted the fender. There is a concrete end result there.

Believe it or not, mechanics are very analytical and have to use a lot of logic and mathematics and physics in their work. Mechanical work is very challenging and I like that. I like to take something that is not functioning, tear it apart, figure out why it's not working, and then fix it. That's sort of what's at the core of Indian intellectualism.

I look at Indian thinking as being a very natural process. That was the approach I took to learning how to become a mechanic. It wasn't linear or strategic. I probably would have struggled to learn mechanics in a classroom. Indian people take this intuitive approach all the time. Whether you call it natural, tactile, visual, or experiential intelligence, we use it for things that are science related, as well as environmental education and learning how to heal someone who is sick. It's just a different style of processing information.

I'm a firm believer in education, despite the tragedy of our past experiences with education. It wasn't until I came to the American Indian College Fund that I found a venue to deal with the historical pattern of abuse and destruction, and of trying to eliminate our culture and essence by whatever possible means. When you look at the turnaround that has taken place since the development of the tribal colleges, you begin to understand the complexity of the historical issues. You also understand that if it weren't for the tribal colleges, we would be a history of people that didn't exist. When these tribal colleges were developed, we took the first steps in turning things around. Indians finally said: "This doesn't work for us. We need to do something different."

We began by doing something different in the classroom. Cultural preservation, tribal governance, all of it, begins with education. It may not have a concrete end to it, but if we could travel forward in time one or two hundred years and were able to look back on the six-hundred-year relationship between Indian people and this country, we could see that the last thirty years have been the most important. It was then that we stopped our extinction and became a factor in determining our own future.

Dr. James **Shanley**

ASSINIBOINE AND SIOUX
PRESIDENT, FORT PECK COMMUNITY COLLEGE
POPLAR, MONTANA

THERE ARE A LOT OF REALLY GOOD INDIAN GOLFERS. I WAS recently at a golf tournament put on by the United Tribes powwow, and they had some of the best Indian golfers there are. I find it to be a tremendous game because it makes you focus, takes your mind off work, and is very challenging. To people who don't play and just see it on TV, it looks fairly simple, but that's because they're watching the best people in the world play. If you go out and actually try to do it, it's very difficult to hit that ball. It's a very humbling game, too, because one day you play really well, and the next day it's like you forgot how to swing. I got started through some people at work who just encouraged me to try it, so I did, and now I try to play as much as I can during the summertime.

This photo is from the annual golf tournament put on by Fort Peck Community College to raise scholarship money for our students, and we've been quite successful at it. We raise about $4,000-$5,000 in scholarships every year. The tournament is very important beyond that, too, because we get many donations from local businesses and individuals. This allows them the opportunity to show their appreciation for the business that we do with them. At the same time, it forces our staff to go out and meet all of the business people who have donated funds to the college.

Last year, we got into a disagreement with the county commissioners over some land at Wolf Point, where we hold the tournament and where I play regularly, about building a new college site there. The entire business community of Wolf Point rallied behind us and more or less helped to persuade the county commissioners to find a suitable alternative place for our new campus. So, doing the tournament and other similar events, things that contribute to the community and that help us interrelate, really strengthens our ability to do what we need to do for the college. A lot of times you don't see those connections. There are more non-Indian people who live in Wolf Point than in any other community on our reservation. If I need to go and talk to somebody in the community, especially if it's somebody I've played golf with, that person is going to talk to me on a different level than if I go in there as a stranger. So that golf tournament has had a lot of benefit.

I don't really think golf is a new or recent phenomenon in Indian communities. I think it's always been there, but perhaps it is more popular now than it's ever been. There are a lot of Indian reservations that have golf courses—either on the reservation or close by. And then, of course, in the Southwest there are now a lot of tribes that have huge, beautiful, tourist-attraction-type golf courses.

Golf is one of those sports that is more appealing later on in life, and so I haven't tried to teach any of my children to play. It's also somewhat expensive, and if you have a young couple or a young person starting out, they usually don't have the time or the money to put into it. Whereas, if they come from a golfing family and they have access to clubs and club memberships and that sort of thing, then there's not much of a problem. Otherwise, it's pretty tough for young people to get into it.

Working at a tribal college is very much like working in politics, in the sense that your day is hardly ever over. If you go downtown and you see people and you visit with people, they're always approaching you with things that they want the college to do, or ideas about how the college can improve, or ways the college should be involved with the tribal government or tribal programs. Any conversation with a tribal councilman always has an improvement agenda. You don't get away from it that much. Sometimes I even get approached about work on the golf course, but I try to avoid that as much as possible.

Dr. Valorie Johnson

EASTERN CHEROKEE, SENECA, AND CAYUGA
PROGRAM DIRECTOR,
W.K. KELLOGG FOUNDATION
BATTLE CREEK, MICHIGAN

I HAVE THE WORLD'S BEST JOB. IT LENDS A LOT OF MEANING to my life because I'm able to use my skills and my education, but also because I have the honor of meeting some of the greatest visionaries there are. These are people from not only tribal colleges and Native groups, but from all different kinds of communities. Sometimes I describe my work as investing in visionaries who want to change the world, and that's what I love about it. Visiting the tribal colleges in particular gives me a lot of hope for the future.

There are so many wonderful ideas and plans for change within the Native community, and people just need resources in order to make things happen. That's where the Kellogg Foundation is able to help. I've seen some incredible projects that have resulted in real positive change for kids, families, and communities.

Before I went to work at the foundation as a program associate, I was the director of Native American Affairs for the state of Michigan. My major concentration was family services and helping Native women get the help they needed to raise their families and to get an education. I was drawn to the mission of the Kellogg Foundation, which is to help people help themselves. I don't really believe in charity for the sake of charity. My job is really about nurturing people to have healthier and more meaningful lives.

I think one of my greatest strengths is that I'm a good persuader. I can convince potential funders to support Native issues, or I can educate my fellow colleagues about the importance of various projects. It opens doors for people. It's not dissimilar from parenting, which I consider the most significant role I've ever had. Family is really important to me, and when I watch my four sons grow and develop, I feel a deep sense of pride. It's also very rewarding because I just love the young men that they have all become. It's one thing to see them mature, but to like the kind of people they have become on top of it, that's really something.

The necklace I'm wearing in the photograph was made by a student at the Institute of American Indian Art (IAIA) in Santa Fe—a beautiful young Mohawk woman named Tsotwew Billings who is learning traditional Iroquois beadworking. I fell in love with the necklace when I saw it at the IAIA Museum market and just started talking to Tsotwew about it. It represents peace and working toward a more tranquil world. I'm proud to wear it because you don't see very much Iroquois beadwork in that style today. In a way, this young artist is reviving an art that not many people can still do.

I come from a whole family of artists. I'm not an artist myself, but art has always played an integral role in my life. Art was what people did in our house, as a living or to make gifts. I did a counseling internship at IAIA when I was in college. It was one of the most eye-opening experiences of my life. I met all of these incredible artists with tremendous talents and was able to experience art firsthand in a new way. And by art, I mean dance, music, fine arts, performance arts, painting, sculpture, and ceramics—just all kinds of creative expression. With all the tribes coming together at that institution to make emerging art, I just thought, "These artists are telling our story better than any term paper or story I could ever write."

People often don't recognize the powerful role that art plays in our communities. Performing art, for example, provides opportunities for reinforcing cultural solidarity and spirituality, and when tribal cultures unite, there is great power. Native arts, in general, reflect the state of our tribal cultures: that's why we see a lot of art that is angry but so much more that portrays beauty. Every year at IAIA, I see incredible artists defining who we are as a people and our ever-changing realities.

I think there is just very little knowledge of the incredible leaders in our community, particularly at the tribal colleges, and the obstacles they are overcoming to create change. I give thanks every day for having had the opportunity to meet so many of them and to witness the work they do with such scarce resources. They need to be supported, and their leadership needs to be recognized and honored, because these individuals are changing the face of Indian education.

Alan **Caldwell**

MENOMINEE

DIRECTOR, CULTURAL INSTITUTE
AND VETERAN'S UPWARD BOUND,
COLLEGE OF THE MENOMINEE NATION
KESHENA, WISCONSIN

AS A TEENAGER GROWING UP ON THE MENOMINEE Reservation in Wisconsin, there weren't many opportunities for sports, especially in the wintertime, other than high school basketball. Boxing was the alternative sport for many of us in our community. Being that I was pretty athletically inclined, I tried out for the boxing team, and I ended up competing in the Wisconsin Golden Gloves Tournament in 1969. In 1973 I was the runner-up in the heavyweight division.

For me, training as a boxer provided an opportunity for physical as well as mental development. It taught me things about discipline and about taking care of my body, and about sportsmanship and competition, and about how to be fair. I incorporated that into my coaching philosophy. As I got more into it, I also became a judge and officiated at many boxing tournaments and shows.

I met a fellow named Vern Woodward, who was the boxing coach at the University of Wisconsin before they dropped the sport back in the mid-1950s. At the time, he was the boxing commissioner for the state of Wisconsin, and he asked me if I would work for his program as an inspector for the state. So anytime there was a boxing show in Wisconsin, I would go as a state representative and make sure that everything was on the up and up—that the coaches, the referee, and the judges were licensed by the Amateur Boxing Federation. If it was professional, I had to make sure that all the boxers were licensed and things of that sort.

Finally, for a couple of years I worked on the promotion side of boxing—I helped to promote shows at the Lac Courte Oreilles Honor the Earth Powwow, the Stockbridge-Munsee Powwow, and I worked with the local teams here at Menominee. So, I've been all over, in all ends of it, and I still maintain an interest in boxing, especially on the amateur level.

I've had health problems over the past few years with diabetes and hypertension and things. I've had open-heart surgery. Since the operation, I've incorporated some of the training for boxing as part of my fitness regimen. I still work out in the garage, where I have a couple of heavy bags, punching bags, as well as jump ropes and things of that sort. A couple of times a week I do my walking and running. By punching bags and skipping rope and doing sit-ups and things like that, I try to help out with those health problems that I've been having recently. I think it's benefited me tremendously as far as my spiritual, mental and physical outlook.

I'm 5'8" and right now I weigh about 220 pounds, but when I was really in it, I weighed about 186, 187 pounds. The fellow who I lost to in that 1973 championship match was a football player from Madison. I still remember his name—Gary Day. He was about 6'2" and weighed maybe 220 pounds. That was a big guy. I think he played linebacker or something for the Badgers, but I wasn't sure of that. I always joke that I didn't know a ring had that many corners in it. That was one of those humbling moments in my life. Because, aside from the beating I got from that fellow—I thought he pushed my nose to the back of my head when he hit me once—I think what hurt more was the fact that three of my sisters were sitting at ringside watching. I think that hurt more than what he did to me.

Della C. Warrior

OTOE-MISSOURIA

PRESIDENT, INSTITUTE
OF AMERICAN INDIAN ARTS
SANTA FE, NEW MEXICO

WE MOVED AROUND A LOT WHEN I WAS GROWING UP—I actually went to six different high schools—and sometimes I wonder how I ever managed to graduate. But I did, and after graduation I went to Cameron Junior College, a small, two-year junior college in Lawton, Oklahoma.

I think there were twelve Indian students at Cameron from throughout the state of Oklahoma, and every day we were bused back and forth between Fort Sill and Cameron. We didn't have a traditional college experience or many interactions with the other college students on campus, mainly because we were brought there in the morning and then picked up at four or five o'clock in the afternoon. If you missed the bus back to Fort Sill, it was quite a ways to walk. We were focused on doing what we were there to do. Although, I recall that one semester we had our own little student protest at Fort Sill. We met with the principal to tell him we wanted to go by the same rules that Cameron had for their freshmen.

Fort Sill had this bell, like a cowbell, and right after dinner they'd ring it and all the girls had to go in. Then they'd ring the bell for lights out. We felt, well, we are college students and we should have the same standards that the freshmen have at Cameron. We were granted that—they got rid of the bell. The other issue was the lunches. They would pack us these sack lunches every day—pork steak, mutton, bologna, or peanut butter and jelly. We protested for a change of menu, and for a while we did get better lunches, but after a couple of weeks it went back to the same old thing.

I suppose that small protest prepared me in some ways for my future, in education and in the work of changing leadership roles for women in Native communities. Obviously, roles for women have changed already, because if you look at the number of women college presidents among the tribal colleges, there are maybe seven or eight; not long ago there were only two or three. Still, women may have unofficial community leadership, but in terms of formalized leadership, it's slower to change. For example, I became the first chairwoman of my tribe's counsel, and many members had a real difficult time accepting a woman in that position. There's always more work to do.

My original goal was to be a medical doctor, and I was on the premed track until my junior year, when I realized that premed was just too difficult given what I was juggling at the time. I had to work to make money, and all the premed courses were solid subjects. I couldn't manage these really hard classes and handle the pressures of a job, too. Before I made that decision, I went to a workshop on American Indian Affairs in Boulder, Colorado. It was a six-week program that brought together thirty-six Indian students from different tribes around the country. It was the first time I'd ever had the opportunity to meet Indian students from places like Alaska, the East Coast, the Northern Plains, and the Southwest. It was a life-changing experience.

The program presented us with information about American Indian policy and the federal government and taught us how to do research and social analysis. We visited different reservations and observed them and then wrote a paper on the communities we had seen. I learned a lot about American Indians and our contributions to mainstream society. Finally, I could start to understand why our people are the way they are—why we can't get jobs and why we have such poverty and drinking problems. There might be an Indian in the kitchen as a cook or in the office as a secretary, but other than that, there were no Indians working in positions of authority or institutional leadership. I just thought, well, there's something very wrong with this. This needs to change, and we can do this. I can do this.

Dr. Carolyn Elgin

CHOCTAW

FORMER PRESIDENT, SOUTHWESTERN
INDIAN POLYTECHNIC INSTITUTE
TALIHINA, OKLAHOMA

RIGHT NOW I'M TRANSITIONING FROM THE STRESS AND responsibility of being a tribal college president to the relative freedom and control I have over my life as a woman in retirement. I do miss the people who I worked with and the students, but I don't miss the traveling. Since I retired, I've enjoyed working on the land around our home—landscaping, tending the flowers, and just being outside in the fresh air.

We literally just cleared a forest. The kids chopped some of the wilderness away around our house—we're trying to tame the land so that we can plant grass, flowers, shrubs, and fruit trees. The vegetation in southeastern Oklahoma is very dense, to say the least, and it's hard to control it because the briars and everything else just want to take over. As soon as you cut them out, they come right back. You have to keep chopping and cutting, bring in a bulldozer and then a brush hog, and finally, you can maintain it with just mowers. Then there's a real sense of satisfaction. Physically, you're tired, but even that feels good sometimes. To be able to look out and think that you moved those rocks or cut those bushes in order to make something your own, well, it's all very beautiful.

I've worked in teaching, counseling, administration, and tribal consulting, but I was the president of Southwestern Indian Polytechnic Institute (SIPI) in Albuquerque for eleven years. My time there provided me with an opportunity to implement some of the programs I felt were necessary to help Indian students succeed in higher education. Tribal colleges are really beneficial for many Indian students who lack the basic skills required and can act as a springboard to go on to major universities, where they can earn higher degrees.

SIPI started as a vocational institution and changed to a two-year associate degree-granting institution, as it remains, in 1993. Prior to that, some of the courses would transfer to a four-year college, but SIPI itself did not grant two-year associate degrees. When I came to the school, I felt it was important for students to have that option. The mission of SIPI became twofold: to prepare students for both a highly technical workforce and a four-year college. It depends on the aspirations of the students, whether they want to go into a program that will lead to a job very quickly or to get their general education requirements taken care of so that they can transfer into a university. The school has tutors, counselors, substance abuse programs, and prevention programs—all so that when students leave SIPI, they're ready and able to join the workforce or to continue with their schooling.

I was born in the Talihina Indian hospital, and my parents purchased this land we now live on when I was about eight years old. Naturally, I feel a strong tie to the land. It's where I grew up, it's where my roots are. It's been wonderful to come back home to live, and it's what I'd actually always planned to do. I never sold the land, because in my heart I always had a desire to return here. It's like a dream come true to be able to live in Oklahoma again after many years of being away. My work was, of course, very satisfying and very rewarding, but I was ready to let someone else take up the banner and to enter into another phase of life.

My husband, Al, is a Pomo from California, and so I was very pleased that he was willing to move here with me, and to call this place his home. He really loves Oklahoma, too. He's a minister and worked as a pastor on several Indian reservations early in his life. Later, he helped to establish many of the urban Indian centers around the country, and he chaired the Task Force for Urban Indians on the American Policy Review. He also worked as executive director of the National Indian Council on Aging, and then from there he went into Indian health care for a number of years. We're both retired now, which is nice. We work side by side, and it was his idea where to put the rose bed this year. It's a pretty spot.

Conrad Fisher

NORTHERN CHEYENNE
DEAN OF CULTURAL AFFAIRS,
CHIEF DULL KNIFE COLLEGE
LAME DEER, MONTANA

THE PHOTOGRAPHER WANTED ME TO BE IN A SETTING OTHER than school where I might be doing one of my hobbies, and I said, "Well, I spend a lot of time here. Here is my hobby." I could've stood by my horses, but I'm not being interviewed based on my horsemanship. I'm here because of this college, and I want to have my picture taken right here on campus.

The Cheyenne people are pretty stubborn. I think a lot of Indian folks have lost not only culture and language, but a way of life and an identity marker about who we are and what we're all about. From a sociological perspective, if you don't have your own identity, you lose confidence, you lose your self-esteem. You just start this downhill spiral because you believe you're not worthy of really anything. You start asking the question, "Who am I?" or "How do I fit in?" or thinking, "I'm not a Cheyenne speaker. What do I know about being a Cheyenne?" You see kids over here who may look Indian, but know nothing about the language or the culture.

And so I think that's really the focus of what I do—educate children and help them to realize that our language and culture are unique to the people who live on this reservation, and that we should be proud of who we really are. We've got such a colorful history—what we stand for and how hard some of our ancestors fought to maintain a way of life and to establish this reservation. The fact that children today know very little about the history of our culture and language really drives what this college stands for.

I went to a boarding school as a child and was taught very little about the Cheyenne culture. Then I went to Eastern Montana College and took some Native American Studies classes. But, like many Indian students, I wasn't ready. At the time, most Indian students just didn't have the support system—parental support, financial support—to deal with college. I spent a year there and then dropped out, or got suspended, actually, for not going to class. I got a lot of Fs.

In short, instead of focusing on college, I got married at a young age, had several kids, took five or six years to mature, and then got to thinking I wanted to go back to school. By that time, my ex-wife and I had gone our separate ways. So I got into the tribal college world. I took some general classes at Dull Knife and then went to Montana State University at Bozeman.

There was one professor at Dull Knife when I was a student here who really helped prepare me for a four-year institution: Will Dowd. He was an English teacher who set a very high standard for being punctual and for the quality of his classes. I think many students rebelled against him because he had such high expectations. He gave me real insight into what a four-year institution would be like. The discipline, and what it takes to be a critical thinker, and to be responsible. I always mention him every place I go because, I don't know, he was a young guy. I think he was just out of college himself, but he really believed in his teaching methods and was committed to bringing them to a tribal college. Ironically, he didn't last very long because there were too many complaints about him and the way he managed his classroom.

I thought about going into social services to help our people back home, but once I graduated from college, I didn't have any clue. I thought about maybe coming back to the tribal college and teaching sociology. Sometimes things just seem to magically appear. There was a position open in a foster-care pilot project, and somebody called me and asked if I wanted to apply for the position, and I got it. Then things started really rolling.

I think we, Chief Dull Knife College and myself, share the same mission, and that is to fight tooth and nail to preserve a way of life among the Northern Cheyenne.

Vernell P. Lane

LUMMI

EXECUTIVE DIRECTOR, NORTHWEST INDIAN COLLEGE
FOUNDATION
BELLINGHAM, WASHINGTON

THE LUMMI RESERVATION IS ON A PENINSULA SURROUNDED by water. Because I was born and raised there, water is an important component in my life. I believe that water has great spiritual significance, and so the beach is a place for me to pray and meditate and clear my head from everyday living. I walk along the beach a lot in the summertime. Sometimes my daughter walks with me, but mostly it's my dog and me.

The house where I grew up is right in front of the rock in this photograph. We swam off of there as kids and spent a lot of time not only on that rock, but also on the beaches around it. We call it Lane Rock. It's actually kind of where we as a family stake our claim. During the summer, when the season is open, we would set out a net as a way of roping off the Lane area.

Water is so important to completing the circle of life. There's an old saying: "When the tide's out, the table is set." One of our elders, Sam Cagey, who passed away, would say this. He meant that when the tide's out, the snipes—the little birds that walk along the beach at low tide—come out to eat. For our people, too, when the tide goes out, we harvest clams, oysters, and horse clams, and all the food that we use to set our table. We feed and nourish ourselves with the seafood that's so important to our diet.

I'm a single mom, and I'm a working mom, and relaxing for me is about getting in touch with myself. That could be sitting on a bench down in the marina. It could be walking in a park. It could be sitting in our church on a Thursday evening just praying to our God. One thing that is really enjoyable for me is talking to our elders. They truly bring out the inner child in me, and it's so comforting to be around them, to eat with them, and to talk with them. I just feel like all my worries are temporarily put aside when I sit down in their house.

Meditation, in whatever form, is for people who do too much. I admit to myself that I'm a woman who does too much. I think a lot of that is because I was raised in a big Catholic family. I'm the sixth of twelve children. The oldest is the queen, she's the boss— what she says goes. The youngest, the baby, always gets her way. Growing up in a huge family, I had to do whatever I could to get what little attention there was to go around. I was also affected by the dysfunction in my family. I had sisters and brothers who ran away, got pregnant, dropped out of high school, and so on. I tried to be "the good daughter," and I think that's what drives me to this day to be as successful as I can be at what I do.

A life-changing experience for me was when I decided to pull canoe for one year in college. I chose to do it because my mom pulled canoe, my grandmother pulled canoe, and when my grandmother and grandfather on my mother's side got married, they were joined in a canoe. When you pull canoe, you can't drink, you can't smoke, and you have to eat a healthy diet. Our elders even say you have to abstain from sex.

When you pull canoe, you're in, let's say, a forty-foot canoe made out of a single cedar tree log. Some of our canoes that we own at Lummi are over seventy-five years old. They each have a significant name—like Setting Sun, Red Wing, or Lone Wolf. It's actually no different than how you would name any pleasure boat or fishing boat, but the spiritual component of climbing into a canoe is, I don't know—words can't even express it, because you're riding in a log from a tree that's so significant to our people. We also use cedar to build our houses, among other things. There's so much that we use of the cedar tree that when you climb into a canoe, it's very intense. It's how I incorporate my culture and who I am into what I do. I wouldn't have it any other way.

Dr. Karen Swisher

STANDING ROCK SIOUX
PRESIDENT, HASKELL INDIAN
NATIONS UNIVERSITY
LAWRENCE, KANSAS

I THINK THERE WERE SOME FEELINGS THAT MAYBE I WASN'T tough enough to do the job as the first woman president of Haskell. My voice is an issue—some people assume that because I have a soft voice, I can't demand the attention I need. I don't believe that's true. I don't think that you need to pound your fists and yell and scream to get your point across. I believe in collaboration and cooperation. I believe in teamwork, and that we all know more collectively than any one of us does individually. I know where the buck stops and I know that I have to make certain decisions, and how I get to those decisions is important to me.

I don't consider myself a pioneer. I'm not a real feminist, but I am very much a believer in equal opportunities. I just believe that women can do anything and should be given the opportunity to live up to their potential, just as men are, so I try to promote women however I can, when appropriate.

I suppose it's one of those indirect teachings, you know, that you don't try to be the center of attention, that if there's any bragging to be done about you, it should be done by somebody else and not yourself. Working hard is important to me. Getting jobs done is important to me. I don't need to be given credit, and that comes from growing up around my family and other people who believe that individual attention, boasting about yourself, or being out there in an inappropriate way should not be encouraged. When it's necessary, I mean, if you are in a leadership position and you must be on stage, or in the spotlight, as they say, by virtue of your position, that's something different.

When I call the tribal office for one reason or another, if the person who answers knows me, they tell me how proud they are of what I'm doing, and I feel good about that. I am pleased that they have confidence in me and my ability. That's the greatest tribute I think anyone could ever have—to be acknowledged in that way by your own people.

All throughout my career as a teacher in higher education, my focus was on teacher preparation. And then I had an epiphany—not only is Indian education important, but teacher education is important to Indian education. It's important how teachers are prepared, because they influence how children learn and help to determine whether students are going to achieve success. In 1994, I came to Haskell during a leave of absence from Arizona State University, where I'd been for nearly ten years, to help in the development of the teacher education program, and I really enjoyed it. I kept in touch with the folks I'd worked with in the following years and came to Haskell permanently in the spring of 1996.

Since being here, I've come to feel that Haskell is just the best there is in Indian higher education. It's hard to communicate the feeling you get when you work at Haskell, or even being here for any length of time. It's a place where you don't have to explain your point of view. You don't have to explain your philosophy because just about everyone here understands the importance of Indian education. You don't have to keep defending what you're doing or why you're doing it, like you do in many of the mainstream colleges and universities.

I love working with young Native students and seeing them have opportunities. I love working with the other tribal colleges and my colleagues there; we are each different, and we each have our own little niche to fill. I feel comfortable coming to the end of my career, because I think the answers to what's ahead in Indian education have been found. When Indians say our children are our future, we say that because we can see our future when we look at these young people getting an education, and it makes us feel good. It makes me feel good. I think one of the benefits of being a woman leader is that there is that sort of matriarchal aspect to it, and that's fun. I was telling somebody recently that I get a lot of hugs in my job, and that's really cool.

Ann Marie Penzkover

LAC COURTE OREILLES OJIBWA

DEAN OF STUDENTS, LAC COURTE
OREILLES OJIBWA COMMUNITY COLLEGE
HAYWARD, WISCONSIN

LIKE THE TRIBAL COLLEGES, AN EXTENDED FAMILY IS BASED on relationships and operates on respect. Hillary Clinton talks about how it takes a village to raise a child, and I think Indians have known that for a long time. My niece Mariah, in the picture with me, is like my own child, and I think in some ways I can be more objective with her than my sister can be. My sister, Nancy, is my best friend. If Mariah has done something a little naughty, Nancy will bring her to me and tell me about it. Then Mariah and I will sit down and discuss what has happened. We've developed a strong respect for each other. It's not just love. It's true respect.

Mariah is just as sweet as she is pretty, and I think that's because her family has made her feel that she is loved. There are many things that will happen in a child's life, so you have to take their little bucket of self-esteem and fill it so full that no matter how many holes are poked in it, there's still enough self-esteem left to get that child through life. I'm all about filling up Mariah's bucket. She's an empowered little eight-year-old girl. She volunteers at school as a leader in her class. She's a peer tutor. I wouldn't have thought of anything like that when I was her age. I guess that's part of what tribal colleges do for people, too—expand our vision for our kids.

My original idea for a career was not so much to go into education, just not to wash dishes for the rest of my life. From about the time I was fourteen years old, I was scrubbing dishes at a truck stop where my mother cooked. Then I became a waitress. Then I was a cook's helper. I saw how hard it was, and how tired my mother would be. I didn't want that life.

My dad worked in construction, and he would come home at night just bone tired. He would sit and grease his hands up, because they would crack and bleed from the work he did, and say to my sister and me: "You kids have to get an education so you don't have to work as hard as I do." He was talking about a high school education with no idea that I would go on to get a college education.

I was the first one in my family to graduate from high school, which was perceived as very honorable. The reaction was a bit different when I got my college degree. I have a big extended family without much education, and my first Christmas home some of them teased me by saying things like: "Well, I suppose you think you're too good for us now," or "I guess we won't see much of you anymore." They really feared that I wouldn't be the same person. It was difficult for them to understand that, yes, a person may change through education, but they don't stop being who they are. After they saw that I wasn't changing and I wasn't going to move away, then they were really proud of me.

I knew there were doctors, lawyers, social workers, and accountants out there—people who worked and paid their bills. It's teaching as a profession that always appealed to me. To be able to take and transmit the culture to the next generation is probably the noblest job there is. I think that the tribal college movement has been the first real opportunity for empowerment for Indian people. From the time students walk through the door, just the improvement in their self-image is amazing. They become actively involved in the community and they want to help validate our culture to the world. There are a lot of people at the tribal colleges who never had a chance to reflect upon their own life. Most of us just go, go, go, but to sit and reflect upon our society, think about our culture and all of the things that go into what we are as people, is rare.

Indian education is a one-to-one relationship for a student. Whether they bond with the recruiter, an instructor, or the janitor they eat lunch with every day, without that individual interaction the education process won't be complete. When I work with students to get them to sign up for school, I spend some time talking with each one. I was a first-generation college student. I didn't know what a credit was either. Now I can sit there with these prospective students and say, "I know what you're going through," because I really do.

John Gritts

CHEROKEE
DIRECTOR, TRIBAL COLLEGE RELATIONS,
AMERICAN INDIAN COLLEGE FUND
DENVER, COLORADO

WHEN I GRADUATED FROM HIGH SCHOOL IN 1966, MY PARENTS told me that if I wanted to go to college, I had three options: Haskell in Lawrence, Kansas; Bacone College in Muskogee, Oklahoma; or the Institute of American Indian Arts (IAIA) in Santa Fe, New Mexico. They offered Haskell because it was run by the Bureau of Indian Affairs and so was free, and Bacone because it was a North American Baptist two-year institution and relatively inexpensive. I don't know how my parents heard about IAIA, but that's where I decided to go.

I never painted with anything other than watercolors, but I was always good at drawing, and I knew how to use colors. My dad was a printer, so I had some slides made of my drawings where he worked to send along with my college application and essay. I think it was late July when I heard from IAIA that I'd been accepted. It was one of the happiest days of my life.

My family is very close-knit. I have four brothers, and my parents have always been very supportive of our choices. Although my brothers and I have all gone in different directions with our careers and so forth, we always manage to come home and spend some time together. I remember the day I left to go to school in Santa Fe—my aunt and uncle drove me because my mom and dad couldn't afford to be away from their jobs. Our family went to church that morning before I left, and to this day that's the only time I can remember seeing my dad cry. I didn't have a girlfriend when I was in high school, and I never went on dates. My best friends were my brothers. All that mattered to me was just hanging out with my family, and then, all of a sudden, I was the first one to leave and go off to school. It was quite an experience.

I remember getting to Santa Fe late at night and not being able to see anything. I had always thought Santa Fe was all desert and cacti— just flat. The next morning I went outside and I just couldn't believe it—there were mountains and trees! It was an incredible sight. I was homesick at first. I didn't quite know how to figure it all out. One time, when I had first gotten there, I went across the street to a little restaurant for lunch. I wasn't feeling well, and the people behind the counter started to ask me questions. I told them that I wasn't feeling very good. "Well," one of them said, "you don't look

like you feel good. Where you from?" I told them I was from Missouri. "Oh," they said, "it's the altitude." They gave me an antacid, and I don't know what it did, but I felt better right away. From that point on, I was never sick from the altitude again.

Gradually, I just started making friends and enjoying what I was doing. Before my first Christmas vacation, I couldn't wait to go home. After a week, once the holiday was over, I was anxious to get back to school. I loved it there.

Indian students who went to IAIA back then had to be from a federally recognized tribe. We weren't allowed to grow our hair long. We had to do jobs. We had curfews. We couldn't leave campus without permission. It's the Army's concept of details. We cleaned the latrines, swept the halls and the stairs, and picked up outside. My first job was working in the cafeteria. I think I had to fry two hundred pork chops on my first day. I learned early on that if you don't ever want to go hungry, work in the cafeteria. The cooks take care of you. When we went to cafeteria in the evenings Monday through Friday, we had to sit family style—boy, girl, boy, girl. They would bring out the food in huge bowls, and we would have to say, "Please pass the mashed potatoes."

I also played in a band at IAIA, and in 1968, *Life* magazine did a spread that included our band, which was quite a coup back then. It was a six-page article, and one of the pictures was of our group, The Jaggers—named after Mick Jagger, of course. I've always loved the Rolling Stones. Although the photo shows me playing a bass guitar, I actually played the organ. We performed at the school dances, and one time we entered a Battle of the Bands and actually won. I spent two years at IAIA. It was a wonderful time. I still smile about it.

Agnes "Oschanee" Kenmille

SALISH

HIDE-TANNING INSTRUCTOR,
SALISH KOOTENAI COLLEGE
PABLO, MONTANA

I LEARNED HOW TO TAN WHEN I WAS FOURTEEN YEARS OLD, in 1932, same year I got married the first time. Didn't even talk to him or anything. We got together and I still didn't talk to him for two days. His family and my family made the arrangement for us to get married. It took two days, and then we finally said, "Hello, how are you doing?"

Been married three times. I was with the first one only a year and half before he passed away. I was with the second one for six years when he got killed at the Kerr Dam. The third one didn't work. I got one daughter and five boys—my daughter is the oldest, she's sixty-six years old. I got over fifty grandchildren. They're still coming.

My first mother-in-law got me started tanning hides. I didn't go to school because I had eczema. She taught me the Kootenai method of tanning and showed me how you scrape the hair off first. It was fresh hide, so I went out and scraped until it was ten inches long and six inches wide. Then I asked her, "Well, how does it look?" and she came in and she said, "It's good. Good work." Since then, I'm tanning hides.

The college built a tanning house for me. I have a big stove in there. The hides got to be warm to tan them. I'm working on four right now. I can do about 200 a year, but I shouldn't do that because I get tired. There's a slaughterhouse here in Ronan that keeps all the hides for me. One time they had 300 for me, 300 deer hides, and I done them all that year.

I use deer brains to tan hides. Yesterday I went to the slaughterhouse and asked them for some brains, and they said they got a couple of bags for me. Gave me, I think, about ten pounds, so I cooked them. I put them all in butter, a little margarine, and then I put it all in the freezer.

Right now I pay twenty dollars to get the hides scraped right because I can't scrape any more. I pay twenty dollars and they still can't do it for me right. If you learn how, you can scrape the hair off in about forty-five minutes. There's a guy from South Dakota who scraped for me all winter, but now he lives in California. He called me here a week ago and asked how I was doing. I'm going to tell him to come back and scrape for me.

I do beadwork, too. My mother taught me when I was young. First thing I beaded was a little, tiny bag shaped like a four-leaf clover. I finished making the bag and told my mother I needed some beads for the background. She said, "Let me see your work." She looked at my work and she said, "Good," and she gave me some red beads. The first time you ever saw a four-leaf clover and it was red. Then I made the background white, and I put in some green leaves. It was the Fourth of July, and this man had a little table where he was selling combs and rings and necklaces, all that cheap stuff, all about a nickel and dime each. He showed me a comb and said, "I'll give you this for your bag." I told him no. He put down a ring, so that would be a comb and a ring for my bag. "No," I told him, "I don't want to." He added a necklace to the spot, a real long necklace, pearl, high-priced pearl—probably worth about fifteen cents at the time—he put that down, too. He had about four or five things on that table. He said, "I'll give you all that for your bag." That was it. Traded my bag for all that stuff.

I've been teaching hide tanning at the college for twenty-two years, but it seems students don't think tanning is fun now. Before, I would have about twenty-four students, but now they sometimes don't all show up. I don't know if they don't want to learn or they found out it's too hard. Yeah, the ways get lost if more don't take the class. But I'll be gone.

Dr. Ron McNeil

STANDING ROCK SIOUX
PRESIDENT AND ALUMNUS,
SITTING BULL COLLEGE
FORT YATES, NORTH DAKOTA

THE MOTORCYCLE. WELL, WHEN I WAS FIFTEEN OR SIXTEEN years old, my brother, my cousins, and friends, we all used to ride dirt bikes. As we got older, we became more interested in larger motorcycles. I began saving money to buy one when I was about eighteen, and when I was twenty I bought my first Harley-Davidson. I remember the exact date: October 14, 1978. I went down to the Harley-Davidson shop in Rapid City, South Dakota, and bought myself one. I'd gone to the Black Hills Motorcycle Rally in Sturgis since I was sixteen, and Harleys were all you ever saw. That was the bike to own and the bike to ride. I've owned a couple of larger Japanese bikes over the years, but those have come and gone. The Harley remains.

I was riding across country with my daughter last summer, and one night we camped overnight in Wyoming. The next morning, we got up early, took baths in the river, and as we were riding down this dirt road to find a place to get breakfast, I just remember feeling so free. I leaned back on the bike, turned my head, and said to my daughter, "My girl, this is the freest I've ever felt."

It was the first bike trip I'd taken with my daughter. We averaged about 270 miles a day. We stopped at all the road signs and historical markers, and we'd never done that before. In a car, you just go right past those markers. When you're riding, you really do get to look around and see much more than you would if you were in a car. We were riding through Yellowstone, and of course all the RVs and cars were in front of us and behind us, and my daughter leaned in and said, "Dad! I see some deer!" And sure enough, in through the trees there was a herd of deer.

In a non-Indian way, I would be the great-great-great-grand-nephew of Sitting Bull. In Indian terms, I would be his great-great-great-grandson. I still haven't come to a complete conclusion about this, but one of the important elements of Sitting Bull's legacy, I think, is his spirituality. Many people have called him a medicine man, but that is a misnomer. He didn't heal people—he prayed, he saw visions, and he shared those visions with others.

When he died, he was brought up to Fort Yates and was actually denied burial in the Catholic cemetery because he hadn't been baptized. He had taken a look at many of the tenets of Catholicism and Christianity, and although in many respects they matched Indian teachings, he never converted. He said once, "What does it matter how I pray, as long as my prayers are answered?" Sitting Bull's legacy on a spiritual level has left our people with the knowledge that our faith is on a par with that of the Europeans.

Another thing that Sitting Bull stood for was resistance to selling our land. He fought against land sale until the day he died. When the land commissioners came, he never signed a treaty. He never, ever, agreed to the termination of ownership of our land. He was not a rich man. He had very little when he died. So, of course, that's also a major part of his legacy—the importance of holding onto our land.

At Sitting Bull College, we don't teach spirituality, but rather, we practice it. You can teach about the ceremonies and the various spiritual elements, which we do, but it's the practicing of it that makes it come alive. The college sponsors weeklong horseback rides that we call Spiritual Rides. I'm given time and financial assistance by the board in order to provide what is needed for the riders and their horses. We have a Wounded Knee ride in December, and another ride in May, right around Memorial Day, where we travel from one known gravesite of a reservation chief to the next in an effort to honor them and the lives they lost. We bring along a drum group, so that we can perform an honor song at each site. The Spiritual Rides are a prominent way that we try to engage the Sitting Bull College students and community with the legacy of Sitting Bull.

I've been asked if motorcycle riding feels anything like horseback riding, and in some ways it does. You cover a lot more ground on a motorcycle, and instead of oats and water, you're looking for gasoline.

A Revolution Comes to Indian Country

BY **SUZETTE BREWER**
CHEROKEE

"Let us put our minds together and see what life we can make for our children."

— **SITTING BULL**, Hunkpapa Lakota

When Don Sam moved to the Flathead Reservation in Montana in the spring of 2000, it was the end of a long journey. At the time, he did not realize that it was also a beginning. A Kootenai tribal member, he had spent most of his childhood being shuffled between non-Indian foster homes, getting in trouble, and feeling angry at the world. He was searching for something different—a life with permanence and continuity. On the Flathead Reservation, Sam got a job working for the Kootenai tribal preservation program and took language lessons at night. At twenty-five, he had some college credits under his belt, though his previous classroom experiences had been largely negative, and he was unfocused about his future. Taking one last crack at earning his degree, he enrolled in Salish Kootenai College in Pablo, Montana, a tribally controlled college. It was a decision that would mark a sea change in his life.

"I came to SKC because of the four-year environmental science program," says Sam, who is now twenty-seven. "But it has changed my whole life and opened up an entirely new world for me, because I now have a purpose and a sense of who I am. Going to college here has been the single most empowering experience of my life—it has allowed me to be the best I can be, and I'd never had that before I came to this college."

Although starting college is a rite of passage for many high school graduates, for Sam and thousands of other young American Indians, higher education is often out of reach. In the thirty-five years since their emergence, however, tribal colleges have come to represent a way out of the poverty and hopelessness that define much of life on the reservations. High unemployment combined with social ills and vast infrastructure needs have caused many Indian people to leave their tribes and families in search of jobs. But for the first time in the history of Indian education, tribal members can now stay home to earn their degrees and remain a part of their communities. The schools have become important hubs in revitalizing native cultures and Indian intellectualism, while helping their communities in such areas as early childhood education, business development, and technology.

After a lifetime of instability and self-doubt, Sam now has hope. He is ready to graduate and expects to go on to a master's degree program. One of his goals is to start his own business someday so that he can employ tribal members. He also was recently elected president of the local chapter of the American Indian Science and Engineering Society, and he completed a ten-week internship with NASA at the University of Maryland in the summer of 2002. Another of his goals is to use Global Information Systems and his environmental training to help his tribe. "Before, I thought, 'NASA, that's for the smart people,'" he says. "But here it was, right in front of me, and the experience made me see what I could do. Now, we're using technology for the benefit of the tribe, because for Indian people it's all about the land."

As a start, Sam has been making maps of the reservation and the United States in the Kootenai language (also known as Ktunaxa, pronounced Too-NAGH-ha), in which he is working hard to become fluent. He is gravely concerned about the future of his culture. "Kootenai is a language isolate—it has no other linguistic relatives," says Sam. "Linguists tell us that it may be extinct by 2017, so it's nice that I can stay home and go to language classes, which we could never do before. In the past, our language was beaten out of us, our culture taken away. And that's the difference a tribal college makes."

"Kill the Indian in him, and save the man."
—**RICHARD PRATT,** Carlisle Indian School, 1888

Tribal colleges were born out of a so-called "Indian education" system that had been a miserable failure. For nearly a century, thousands of Indian children were forcibly taken by agents from their homes in government roundups and sent to faraway government boarding schools where they had their long hair cut off, were dressed in military-style uniforms, and were forbidden to speak their languages or practice their Native religions. As wards of the state, many tried to run away, became ill, or died under mysterious circumstances. Those who survived found it hard to return home because they felt like outcasts in their own communities.

Discipline at these schools was harsh, as their primary mission was the forcible assimilation of Indian children into the white man's world. Many boys and girls were beaten or had their mouths washed with lye soap for speaking their Native languages. Some were forced into hard labor with no real education or job training. Boarding schools left physical and emotional scars on the students, who, after becoming parents themselves, were often leery of the concept of "education" for their own children. They refused to teach their languages and cultural practices for fear that their sons and daughters would receive the same treatment. As a result, hundreds of Native languages, oral histories, and religious practices became either extinct or endangered within two generations. But in the mid-twentieth century, things began to change.

With their cultures in jeopardy and their economies in shambles, Indians knew that the best hope for improvement would come from within their own community. The government had broken every treaty made with Indian tribes and had reneged on promises made in exchange for the vast forfeiture of land and natural resources. Characterized as the "Forgotten Americans" by President Lyndon Johnson, Indian people languished in extreme poverty in remote regions with no hope of recovering all that had been lost.

During the 1960s, the Civil Rights Movement was in full swing and American Indian activism was taking hold in tribes across the country. For centuries, Indian people had struggled against near annihilation, forced assimilation, and relocation. Now they were beginning to take control of their own destinies.

Education would become the critical component in reshaping Indian communities. Centuries earlier, tribal leaders had known and understood that education would be the foundation of Indian survival and had negotiated for the schooling of their children in nearly every treaty with the government. But as the government sought to "de-Indianize" the Indian in the classroom, low self-esteem and poor educational attainment rates among generations of students began to soar.

David Gipp had a front-row seat to the activism and change of the 1960s. As a boy growing up in the Dakotas, he could not envision the revolution in Indian country that was about to take place—the tribal college movement. An enrolled member of the Standing Rock Sioux Tribe, he had attended school at Saint Paul's Catholic Indian Mission in Yankton, South Dakota, and knew first hand the boarding school experience. In the late 1960s, he and his Indian colleagues, all young and well educated, quickly realized that this new way of teaching Indian people would be different and more successful than anyone in Indian education could have ever anticipated. At the same time, they knew that finding long-term support would be an uphill struggle. Eventually, however, many in the Indian community realized that for their people to survive, they had to become lawyers, educators, and activists themselves—to work within a system that had failed them for so long.

"We walked into an era when change was being promoted in the Indian community," says Gipp. "There was change in education, change in politics, change in tribal governments, and we had no frame of reference for what was happening, so we had to redefine everything as we went along. It was an exciting time."

In 1968, the Navajo Nation took the lead by founding the Navajo Community College, now known as Diné College, in Tsaile, Arizona. As America's first and largest tribally controlled institution of higher learning, it was the flagship school full of possibility and hope for Indian people. Other tribes immediately took notice and began making plans to start their own colleges. Members of reservation communities gathered in living rooms and backyards to form ad hoc committees and to lay out their plans.

With no money, and inadequate equipment, staff, and facilities, five other colleges soon followed: Oglala Lakota College in Pine Ridge, South Dakota; Sinte Gleska University in Rosebud, South Dakota; Sitting Bull College in Fort Yates, North Dakota; Turtle Mountain Community College in Belcourt, North Dakota; and D-Q University in Davis, California. The schools were set up in abandoned houses, trailers, old storefronts, condemned buildings, barracks, and warehouses—any structure where students and teachers could gather for classes. Often, students studied in their cars because there was no place on campus with heating.

"In the early days, when we had meetings, we literally held hands and prayed, because we had nothing else," says Carol Davis, who is now vice president of Turtle Mountain. "We had no money and no equipment, so in the beginning we just prayed that the money would come in."

With the passage of the Indian Self-Determination Act and the Indian Education Act in the 1970s, the government began to acknowledge that tribes were better off making decisions about education for themselves. Tribes were now able to contract for local schools on their reservations, and many Indians began attending mainstream colleges. But many students were compelled by cultural and social stress to drop out and return home as casualties of the white man's educational system. Some, however, chose to complete their education and return to the reservation and try to change the system. Slowly, more tribal colleges began to appear on reservations. It was the beginning of a movement that would have far-reaching implications for Indian communities across the United States.

After all, these schools were no ordinary, run-of-the-mill community colleges. In an unprecedented way, tribes determined what was important; they helped define the mission, direction, and focus of the colleges, at the same time working to help incorporate and emphasize tribal values, language, and culture into every area of the curriculum. For example, students in science were now taught the English, Latin, and Indian language name of a particular plant or constellation and its uses in both mainstream and Indian culture. Learning Indian history and oral traditions became just as important as studying ancient Greece or Egypt. The Indian perspective would no longer take a backseat to Western culture.

"We were the new kids on the block," says Gipp. "But we found out in no time flat that we had to break open the door because it was closed to us. We had to figure out how to last beyond the next paycheck and how to get accreditation. We needed long-term financial support."

In the early 1970s, the original six tribal colleges were operating—and seeking funding—independently, with no real cohesive goals or unified objectives. But eventually leaders from the six schools joined forces and created the American Indian Higher Education Consortium (AIHEC) to advance the collective agenda of the schools. Funding, accreditation, research, and cooperative education were among the organization's areas of emphasis. In the fall of 1973, AIHEC opened its offices in Denver, Colorado, with Gipp as its first executive director.

"I majored in political science and I never envisioned myself in Indian higher education, because prior to that time there was nothing to envision—because it didn't exist," he says. "But there was definitely a sense of excitement and newness and creation because it was something that belonged to us, and to me, that is the fundamental purpose of our mission."

Gipp is now president of United Tribes Technical College in Bismarck, North Dakota, an institution jointly owned by all the North Dakota tribes and the Sisseton-Wahpeton Band of Sioux in South Dakota. AIHEC has since relocated to Washington, D.C., and continues its lobbying efforts on Capitol Hill on behalf of the tribal colleges.

> "The life of a man is a circle from childhood to childhood and so it is in everything where power moves."
> —**BLACK ELK**, Oglala Lakota

Since the appearance of tribal colleges in the late 1960s, the lives and communities of Indian people have changed forever. These institutions have been developed by and for Indian communities, providing excellent higher educational opportunities while reinvigorating the cultures from which they come. For the first time in a long and painful history of Indian education, there is hope.

Today, there are thirty-two tribal colleges in twelve states, from California to Michigan and from Arizona to North Dakota. More than 30,000 students are enrolled from more than 250 tribes and indigenous groups across the United States and Canada.

In 1989, the member institutions of AIHEC formed the American Indian College Fund as a separate fundraising entity to seek private money for scholarships, endowments, and developmental needs at the tribal colleges. Since its inception, the Denver-based College Fund has given more than $23 million in scholarships to thousands of American Indian students, who are among the poorest in the nation. Additionally, the organization underwrites programs in teacher training, cultural preservation, capital construction, business development, and technology at the tribal colleges. It is the largest nonprofit provider of scholarships to American Indian students in the country.

"Tribal colleges have changed the history of Indian education in America," says Richard B.

Williams, executive director of the College Fund since 1997. "Indian people are now excited about learning, excited about going to class, and proud of who they are and where they come from. It's wonderful to see such a dramatic change in a lifetime."

The colleges have been successful because they have adapted their curriculums and services to reflect the values, traditions, and intelligence of Indian people. They have provided a safe educational experience that supports Indian learning styles and fosters an environment of respect and cultural sensitivity. The mission of the American Indian College Fund is to ensure that the needs of the colleges and their students are met, while educating the public about the schools' successes with Indian students, their broader impact on Native American communities, and their effect on the entire country. In a twist of the Indian Relocation policies of the 1960s, American Indian students living in urban areas are now choosing to "return home" to attend tribal colleges as their first choice, says Williams. "There they can learn about their culture, history, and languages without feeling like they're on the outside," he says. "At the same time, students can obtain a degree that will allow them to achieve their higher education goals and go on to help their communities."

Thanks to the vision and hard work of the tribal colleges, degree-attainment rates are rising among American Indian students. Educators know that a strong sense of identity and self-respect is critical to any student's success in learning. At tribal colleges, administrators and teachers reinforce the students' tribal associations while providing them with resources, skills, and education for a lifetime. Students are encouraged to learn about other tribes' histories and cultures as well as their own. Tribal colleges have not only changed the history of Indian education, but also their communities for generations to come.

For students like Don Sam, it couldn't have come a moment too soon. "Going to my own tribal college is deep—it's a part of me," he says. "When I was in tenth grade, I thought I'd be lucky if I were alive in five years. Now, to be considering graduate school is amazing to me. Learning to speak the language of science and forestry and archaeology and being able to bring that to my community is so empowering because it helps to build that bridge for my people. It's made me a better person, and for that I'm deeply grateful."

"If the Great Spirit had desired me to be a white man he would have made me so in the first place. He put in your heart certain wishes and plans; in my heart he put other and different desires. Each man is good in the sight of the Great Spirit."

—**SITTING BULL,** Hunkpapa Lakota

Subject Biographies

BENJAMIN BARNEY, Navajo, is the director of the Center for Diné Teacher Education at Diné College in Tsaile, Arizona. Barney received his bachelor's degree from St. John's College in Santa Fe, New Mexico, and his master's degree from the University of New Mexico. He has an interest in dance and has studied modern dance, ballet, jazz, folk, and Indian dance forms throughout the United States and Europe. His career has focused on education at the Navajo Reservation, in places such as the Rough Rock Demonstration School and other educational institutions. He has consulted for the Arizona Commission on the Arts, Freiburg Teachers Institute, Hinterzarten, Germany, and other educational institutions. He is a member of many boards, including Lok'aa'ch'égai Community Education and the Smithsonian Indian programs, and he has traveled worldwide.

DENNIS BERCIER, Turtle Mountain Band of Chippewa, is a North Dakota state senator and a former student of Turtle Mountain Community College in Belcourt, North Dakota. He was a high school dropout who joined the U.S. Army during the Vietnam War. Elected in 1999, he is the fourth Indian legislator in the history of North Dakota. He received his B.A. from the University of North Dakota. He owns several businesses and works in institutional resource development for Turtle Mountain Community College.

ALAN CALDWELL, Menominee and White Earth and Mille Lacs Ojibwa, is the director of the Culture Institute and Veteran's Upward Bound at the College of the Menominee Nation, Keshena, Wisconsin. He received his master's degree from the University of Wisconsin-Madison and his bachelor's degree from the University of Wisconsin-Green Bay. He is a former Indian education specialist for the Wisconsin Department of Public Instruction, as well as a U.S. Army veteran who served in Vietnam.

MARGARETT CAMPBELL, Assiniboine, is the vice president of Community Services at Fort Peck Community College, Poplar, Montana. Prior to this position, she served as president of Fort Belknap College, Harlem, Montana for nine years. Campbell has A.A., B.S., and M.S. degrees from Northern Montana College, Havre, Montana, and is working on her Ph.D. at the University of Montana. She is a board member of the Montana Civil Liberties Union and president of the Montana Indian Education Association. Campbell chaired the U.S. Department of Agriculture committee responsible for research and development of legislation for the tribal colleges and universities "Equity in Educational Land-Grant Status Act of 1994."

ALPHONSO COLEGROVE, Hoopa Valley and Yurok, is a graduate of Northwest Indian College in Bellingham, Washington. He was the president of the college's student council, president of the American Indian Higher Education Consortium Student Congress, Student of the Year for Northwest Indian College, and President of Beta Theta Beta of Phi Theta International Honor Society. While at Northwest Indian College, Colegrove worked as an unpaid intern, volunteer, computer technician assistant, and a contractor. He also worked as an intern for Allstate Insurance Company in Northbrook, Illinois, for two summers and designed the data engineer project as a program for tribal college students and employees.

VINE DELORIA JR., Standing Rock Sioux, is an author and historian. He is a retired professor and adjunct professor at the University of Colorado and the University of Arizona. He obtained a master of theology degree from the Lutheran School of Theology in Rock Island, Illinois, in 1963 and a J.D. from the University of Colorado in 1970. He is a veteran of the U.S. Marine Corps. He received the Center of the American West's Wallace Stegner Award, an honor bestowed each year on someone who has made a sustained contribution to the cultural identity of the West. He is one of the most outspoken figures in Native American affairs. He also sits of the board of the Smithsonian's National Museum of the American Indian. His works promote Native American cultural nationalism and a greater understanding of Native American history and philosophy. Deloria has been an ardent supporter of the tribal college movement from the beginning. From 1964 to 1967, he served as the executive director of the National Congress of the American Indians.

DR. CAROLYN ELGIN, Choctaw, recently retired as president of Southwestern Indian Polytechnic Institute (SIPI) in Albuquerque, New Mexico. Elgin earned her Ed.D. in educational administration from the University of New Mexico, and her M.A. and B.A. degrees from California State University, Sacramento. Under Elgin's leadership, SIPI has evolved from offering vocational-technical courses to granting associate of applied science, associate of arts, and associate of science degrees. Under Elgin's leadership since 1991, the college, which one congressman last year called "the jewel of New Mexico," has become renowned for providing quality education to American Indians and Alaska Native Americans.

CONRAD FISHER, Northern Cheyenne, is the dean of Cultural Affairs at Chief Dull Knife College, Lame Deer, Montana. Fisher graduated from Montana State University at Bozeman with his B.A. degree. He served on the tribal council for two terms. Fisher received the Phyllis Berger Outstanding Leadership Award from the American Indian Club at Montana State University. He is a fluent speaker of the Northern Cheyenne language and has directed a language immersion program at the college. He is a member of the Omaha Society (drumkeeper) within the tribe and a member of the Montana Historical Preservation Review Board.

DR. DAVID M. GIPP, Standing Rock Sioux, is president of United Tribes Technical College in Bismarck, North Dakota. He received his B.A. from the University of Mary, and doctor of laws, honoris causa, from North Dakota State University. He also received the Martin Luther King, Jr. Award for Multicultural Education from the U.S. Department of Public Instruction and the Educator of the Year Award from the National Indian Education Association. Prior to his presidency, Gipp was the executive director of the American Indian Higher Education Consortium and executive director of the Office of Tribal Management and Budget for the Standing Rock Sioux Tribe.

DR. GUY GORMAN SR., Navajo, is known as the "father of the tribal college movement" and one of the cofounders of Navajo Community College, now Diné College. Gorman grew up in Bureau of Indian Affairs schools at home and finished school at Chilocco Indian School in Oklahoma. He was drafted for the service, serving for four years. Upon returning home, he was employed by the Bureau of Indian Affairs, and in 1962 he was elected as council delegate for the Chinle Chapter and served on the Navajo Nation Council Education Committee as vice-chairman. Under his vision, the first contract school was established by the Snyder Act, which allowed the Rough Rock Demonstration School to be administered by the first all-Navajo board of directors. At this school, the first Navajo language and culture courses were infused into the regular curriculum. His work in education continued as he led the effort to establish Navajo Community College, the first tribally controlled higher education institution in the United States. He served as chair of the first Navajo Community College Board of Regents.

JOHN GRITTS, Cherokee, is the director of tribal college relations for the American Indian College Fund. Gritts graduated from the Institute of American Indian Arts in Santa Fe, New Mexico, and Bacone College in Muskogee, Oklahoma, and has his B.A. from Sioux Falls College, Sioux Falls, South Dakota. He was the director of financial aid at Black Hills State University for over 16 years. He personally presented President Jimmy Carter with a piece of his artwork on behalf of the state of South Dakota in 1976.

MARITA HINDS, Tesuque Pueblo, is the major gifts officer at the Institute of American Indian Arts development office. Prior to this position, Hinds was the special projects coordinator at the Institute of American Indian Arts Museum. She is an alumna of the Institute of American Indian Arts with an A.F.A., and earned her B.A. from the College of Santa Fe. During her career, she has helped curate many art shows at the museum and other galleries, as well as served on several educational and art organizations and boards.

TRACEY JILOT, Chippewa-Cree, is head librarian at Stone Child College, Rocky Boy Agency, Montana. Jilot started her college classes at Stone Child College and earned her B.A. degree from Northern Montana College in Havre, Montana. Prior to attending college, she was a daycare provider on the reservation. Upon graduating, she returned to Stone Child College as a chemical dependency counselor before overseeing the library. She was chosen Outstanding College Student of the Year by her tribe and was an honor student all four years at Northern Montana. At Stone Child she was a member of the student senate, academic challenge team, and basketball team.

DR. VALORIE JOHNSON, Eastern Cherokee, Seneca, and Cayuga, is a program director for the W.K. Kellogg Foundation. Previously, Johnson was director of Native American Affairs for the state of Michigan's Department of Social Services in Lansing. Johnson began her career as a human relations executive with the National Education Association in Washington, D.C. She earned her Ph.D. from Michigan State University, and her M.Ed. and B.S. degrees from the University of Hawaii. She also served as a guidance counselor at the Institute of American Indian Arts in Santa Fe, New Mexico, and the Kamehameha Schools in Honolulu, Hawaii. She formerly served on the board of regents for Bay Mills Community College and now serves on the board of Americans for Indian Opportunity. Her leadership with the W.K. Kellogg Foundation's Native American Higher Education Initiative has elevated the tribal colleges to a new level.

AGNES "OSCHANEE" KENMILLE, Salish, is a semiretired and part-time instructor at Salish Kootenai College in Pablo, Montana, where she has taught since the college was established. The college student services building is named after her. She teaches the traditional way of tanning hides and also tans over 200 deer hides at home, as well as doing beadwork. She is fluent in both Salish and Kootenai languages, culture, and traditions. Kenmille also teaches at the tribal high school. She serves as the lady war dance chief for the Salish Indians. She is well respected throughout the northwest; her beaded moccasins, gloves, and vests are treasured and worn proudly by people throughout the region.

CARLY KIPP, Blackfeet, a graduate of Blackfeet Community College in Browning, Montana, is now enrolled at the University of Great Falls, Great Falls, Montana, majoring in biology with plans to become a veterinarian. While at Blackfeet Community College, she was certified by the state of Montana to tutor students with learning disability problems. She also worked as a peer tutor at the college and as a field technician who documented the tribal buffalo herd and native plants and animals. Kipp was the American Indian Higher Education Consortium Student of the Year. She was also named Outstanding Science Student and a Gates Millennium Scholar. Kipp is featured in the American Indian College Fund's new ad campaign.

VERNELL P. LANE, Lummi, is the executive director of the Northwest Indian College Foundation. She graduated with an A.A.S. degree from Northwest Indian College, and received her B.A. from Western Washington University in Bellingham, Washington. She also has an M.A. from Seattle University, Seattle, Washington. Her background is in land acquisition and tribal planning. She has participated in the Lummi Health and Economic Commission, the Boys and Girls Club, and Lummi Veterans program planning. She is a board member of the Washington Children's Alliance.

DR. ELDEN LAWRENCE, Sisseton-Wahpeton Sioux, is the recently retired president of Sisseton Wahpeton College (FKA Sisseton Wahpeton Community College) in Sisseton, South Dakota. He attended a township country school and one year of government boarding school before enlisting in the U.S. Army at age seventeen. He received his A.A. degree from Sisseton Wahpeton Community College, his B.S. degree from Moorhead State University, his M.A. from the University of South Dakota, and is only the second Native American to earn a Ph.D. from South Dakota State University. He was honored by South Dakota State University with the distinguished Native American Alumni Award. His hometown of Peever honored him as the grand marshall of a Norwegian parade. He was a member of the public school board in Sisseton, South Dakota.

DR. JOSEPH MCDONALD, Salish Kootenai, is one of the founders of Salish Kootenai College in Pablo, Montana, and has served as its president since 1978. In 1989, he was named the National Indian Education Association's Indian Educator of the Year. In 1999, he was named a member of the Board of Advisors on Tribal Colleges and Universities. He has served on numerous boards, including the Ford Foundation, the Carnegie Foundation, the American Indian College Fund, the American Indian Higher Education Consortium, and the national advisory board for the Boyer Center. From 1968 to 1976, he served as a high school principal and assistant superintendent in Ronan, Montana. He later created the first Native American Studies program in Montana public schools. McDonald received his associate degree and teaching certificate from Western Montana College, and his B.S., M.S., and Ph.D. degrees from the University of Montana.

DR. RON MCNEIL, Standing Rock Sioux, is the great-great-great-grandson of Chief Sitting Bull. He is an alumnus and president of Sitting Bull College in Fort Yates, North Dakota. Under his tenure, the campus formally changed its name from Standing Rock College to Sitting Bull College. He is a graduate of the University of South Dakota School of Law. Prior to his tenure at Sitting Bull College, McNeil was the executive director of the American Indian College Fund. He worked in a private law practice in South Dakota before turning his professional interest to Indian education. McNeil has been appointed as Chairman to President George W. Bush's board of advisors for the Whitehouse Initiative on Tribal Colleges and Universities.

JARETT D. MEDICINE ELK, Northern Cheyenne and Assiniboine, graduated with an associate of science degree in general studies from Fort Peck Community College. He served as student body government president while at Fort Peck. Medicine Elk is featured in the American Indian College Fund's new ad campaign. He is a member of the American Indian Higher Education Consortium Student Congress. He recently completed two internships with Allstate Insurance Company.

DR. GERALD "CARTY" MONETTE,
Turtle Mountain Band of Chippewa, is
one of the founding fathers of the tribal
college movement and of the American
Indian Higher Education Consortium.
He is the president of Turtle Mountain
Community College in Belcourt, North
Dakota. Monette serves as a member
of the National Advisory Group to the
Institute of Higher Education's New
Millennium Project; of the National
Agriculture Research, Extension, and
Economics Advisory Board; and a member
of the North Dakota Information
Technology Council. Monette received a
B.A. degree from Mayville State College,
and M.A. and Ed.D. degrees from the
University of North Dakota.

SHEILA M. MORRIS, Omaha, is an alumna
of Nebraska Indian Community College
(NICC) in Winnebago, Nebraska, with an
A.A. degree, and is currently working as
an administrative assistant for the Omaha
Alcohol Program. At the urging of then
college president Thelma Thomas, she
went back to school at age thirty-eight,
a mother of seven children. She went
on to become student senate president,
American Indian Higher Education
Consortium Student of the Year for the
college, a peer counselor, and the student
advisor for NICC's reaccreditation visit.
She worked as the site coordinator of the
Macy campus and later the site coordinator
for the Sioux City campus.

LES NORTHRUP SR., Fond du Lac Band
of Lake Superior Chippewa, is the chief
security officer and recruiter at Fond du
Lac Tribal and Community College. He
has his A.A. degree from Fond du Lac
Tribal and Community College and his
B.S. degree from the University of
Minnesota-Duluth. The college created
the Les Northrup Award, presented annually
to an outstanding student in law enforcement, in his honor. He serves on several
committees, including the Arrowhead Area
Agency for Aging, Arrowhead Regional
Development Commission and Board
of Directors, and Arrowhead Economic
Opportunity Agency Board of Directors.

GERALD ONE FEATHER, Oglala Lakota,
is a lifetime advocate of higher education
for the Lakota people. He graduated from
the University of South Dakota with his
B.A. degree and attended graduate school
at the University of Oklahoma. One
Feather is one of the founders of Oglala
Lakota College and now serves as a member
of the Elder Advisory Committee for the
college. He was the president of Oglala
Sioux Tribe in 1970 and served as the
president of the United Sioux Tribes.
In 1972, he developed the Center for
Indian Studies at Black Hills State College
in Spearfish, South Dakota. Recently
Oglala Lakota College has established the
Gerald One Feather Lakota Studies Faculty
Endowment Fund in his honor.

DR. JANINE PEASE-PRETTY ON TOP,
Crow, served as president of Little Big
Horn College in Crow Agency, Montana,
until 2001. She began her education career
in the 1970s as a counselor for Navajo
Community College and as director of
the Crow adult and vocational programs.
Later, she served as director of Indian
Career Services at Eastern Montana
College. Pease-Pretty On Top was named
Indian Educator of the Year by the
National Indian Education Association
in 1990 and received a MacArthur
Foundation "genius" grant in 1994. She
was named to the National Advisory
Council on Indian Education by presidential
appointment. She received her B.A.
from Central Washington University and
her M.A. and Ed.D. from Montana State
University in 1994. Pease-Pretty On Top is
the first Crow woman to earn a doctorate.

ANN MARIE PENZKOVER, Lac Courte Oreilles Band of Lake Superior Chippewa, is the dean of students at Lac Courte Oreilles Ojibwa Community College, Hayward, Wisconsin. Penzkover has an A.A. degree from the University of Wisconsin-Barron County, Rice Lake, Wisconsin, a B.S. from the University of Wisconsin-River Falls, Wisconsin, and another B.S. and M.S. degree from the University of Wisconsin-River Falls. Prior to her current position, she worked in South Dakota and Minnesota in education-related jobs. Among her many affiliations, she is a member of the American Society of Composers, Authors, and Publishers; Laubach Literacy Action International; and the Lac Courte Oreilles Girl Scouts.

JUAN PEREZ, Klamath and Modoc, is currently working at Salish Kootenai College as Student Life and Athletics Coordinator. He served in the U.S. Army and was sent overseas during the Persian Gulf War, where he was stationed in Germany at a receiving hospital for casualties. After serving, he enrolled at Salish Kootenai College and received his B.A. degree in Native American human services. Perez was an ambassador for the American Indian Higher Education Consortium (AIHEC), and went to Sarajevo in the summer of 2001 to speak about Native American people and experiences. He is a former AIHEC Student Congress president.

DR. LANNY REAL BIRD, Crow, is the director of the Learning Lodge Institute at Little Big Horn College in Crow Agency, Montana. He has worked at the college for over a decade. Real Bird received his B.A. from Eastern Montana College and his M.A. and Ed.D. degrees from Montana State University at Bozeman. His doctorate thesis was titled upon his own Crow (Apsaalooke) culture: "Ashaammaliaxxia, the Apsaalooke Clan System: A Foundation for Learning." Real Bird considers himself a practicing nativist and participates in the traditional practices of the Apsaalooke. He had also taught Plains sign language at an early age. While spending time with the Hidatsa, he acquired some fluency in that language as well.

DAVID RISLING, Hoopa Valley, Karuk, and Yurok, is a retired director and professor of Native American studies at the University of California, Davis and one of the founders and original board members of D-Q University in Davis, California. He helped to create and manage numerous state and national organizations dedicated to promoting and protecting Native American legal, economic, and social interests. After military service with the Naval Reserves, Risling earned his B.A. from California State Polytechnic University. He earned his M.A. degree from California State University. Risling has served on the board of the National Indian Education Association and assumed leadership roles with the Association on American Indian Affairs and the Native American Rights Fund. He was awarded the UC Davis Distinguished Public Service Award.

DR. JAMES SHANLEY, Assiniboine and Sioux, is president of Fort Peck Community College in Poplar, Montana. He is a Vietnam War veteran, an educator, and leader of the American Indian Higher Education Consortium (AIHEC). Shanley earned his B.A. degree from Eastern Montana College, his M.A. from Arizona State University, and his Ph.D. from the University of North Dakota. Shanley has published studies and evaluations of Indian education since 1972, including some of the most comprehensive research about Indian education. During Shanley's first term as president of the board of directors of AIHEC in 1978, he provided substantial work and leadership in securing the passage of the Tribally Controlled Community College Act.

VANESSA SHORTBULL, Oglala Lakota, is the daughter of Tom and Darlene Shortbull. Her father serves as president of Oglala Lakota College in Kyle, South Dakota. Shortbull attended Oglala Lakota College and has her B.A. from the University of South Dakota. She was named Miss South Dakota and represented the state at the Miss America Pageant in Atlantic City, New Jersey, in 2002. In 2001, she was Miss South Dakota State Fair and the first Native American to win the pageant. She is scheduled to appear in the next round of American Indian College Fund ads. Shortbull is also a stand-up comic and was one of the finalists for the Four Directions NBC talent search competition.

DR. KAREN SWISHER, Standing Rock Sioux, is the first woman president to head Haskell Indian Nations University. She joined Haskell in 1996 to direct its teacher training program and chair its teacher education department. Swisher has a B.A. and M.S. from Northern State University in Aberdeen, South Dakota. She also has her Ed.D. from the University of North Dakota. She has been active in numerous education organizations, including the National Indian Education Association (NIEA) and the American Educational Research Association. She has served on the boards of the Urban Indian Education Research Center, the American Indian College Fund, and Girl Scouts of the USA. In 1997 she received the NIEA's highest award, Indian Educator of the Year, and in 1998 was named Native American Educator of the Year by the Kansas Association for Native American Education. Swisher has been appointed to President George W. Bush's board of advisors for the White House Initiative on Tribal Colleges and Universities.

WADE I. TEEPLE, Bay Mills Indian Community, is currently the off-campus coordinator/contracts grants officer at Bay Mills Community College in Brimley, Michigan. He attended Bay Mills Community College and the U.S Indian Police Academy. Teeple served in the 101st Airborne Division-ETS, has been a commercial fisherman, was a tribal police officer, and served as tribal chairman when the community college was established.

DELLA C. WARRIOR, Otoe-Missouria, is president of the Institute of American Indian Arts in Santa Fe, New Mexico. She has helped the college become financially stable, securing two-year and four-year accreditation and leading the effort to build the college a permanent home on a 140-acre campus. She earned her B.A. at Northeastern State University in Tahlequah, Oklahoma, and her M.S. from Harvard. She is currently working on her Ph.D. from the University of New Mexico. She has been the only woman to serve as chairperson and CEO of her tribe. Warrior is a board member of the National Museum of the American Indian at the Smithsonian Institution and the American Indian Higher Education Consortium. She was appointed to President George W. Bush's board of advisors for the White House Initiative on Tribal Colleges and Universities.

MARVIN B. WEATHERWAX, Blackfeet, is the Blackfeet Studies department chair at Blackfeet Community College in Browning, Montana. He was a prisoner of war during the Vietnam War and has gone on to become a film producer and a cultural elder. He has an A.A. degree from Blackfeet Community College and a B.A. degree from Eastern Washington University in Cheney, Washington. He is working on his M.A. degree from Harvard. He has been working with linguists from the Ukraine and France and has been helpful in teaching the Blackfeet language. He created a series of videotapes and audiotapes to teach the language, and he works with the Learning Lodge Institute language immersion camps. He was honored by students and peers as Teacher of the Year at Blackfeet Community College.

RICHARD B. WILLIAMS, Oglala Lakota,
is the executive director of the American
Indian College Fund. Prior to coming
to the College Fund, he was director of
the Student Academic Service Center at
the University of Colorado in Boulder,
Colorado. Previously he served as director of
Minority Student Affairs, director of the
American Indian Upward Bound Program,
and director of the TRIBES program.
Williams received his B.A. from the
University of Nebraska–Lincoln and his M.A.
from the University of Wyoming.
In April 1999, the University of Nebraska
honored Williams with the Distinguished
Alumni Award. Williams has been appointed to
President George W. Bush's board of advisors
for the White House Initiative on Tribal
Colleges and Universities.

America's Tribal Colleges

BAY MILLS COMMUNITY COLLEGE

Bay Mills Community College is located inside the boundaries of the Bay Mills Indian Community on the eastern Upper Peninsula of Michigan. It provides education for most of the Michigan reservations and is part of the larger Chippewa or Ojibwa population in the region. Bay Mills was first accredited by the North Central Association of Colleges and Schools in 1995.

BLACKFEET COMMUNITY COLLEGE

Founded in 1974, Blackfeet Community College was the first tribal college in Montana. On December 11, 1985, it became a fully accredited institution. The college is located in Browning, Montana, on the Blackfeet Indian Reservation, where the mountains meet the plains of northern Montana.

CANKDESKA CIKANA COMMUNITY COLLEGE

Cankdeska Cikana Community College was founded in October 1974. The college serves the residents and communities on and near the Spirit Lake Indian Reservation, Fort Totten, North Dakota. It was named in honor of Cankdeska Cikana (meaning "Little Hoop"), the Indian name of Paul Yankton, Sr. PTF Yankton, the recipient of two Purple Hearts, who died November 29, 1944, while serving as a rifleman with the Army's 11th Infantry at Larraine, France. In 1981, Cankdeska Cikana Community College initiated the accreditation process and became accredited by the North Central Association of Colleges and Schools in February 1990.

CHIEF DULL KNIFE COLLEGE

The college is named after Chief Dull Knife, also known as Morning Star, who, under great odds and with great courage, led his band of Northern Cheyenne to their homeland in 1884. Reflecting Chief Dull Knife's determination, the college's primary mission is to provide educational and cultural leadership to its constituents. Chief Dull Knife College, in Lame Deer, Montana, was chartered in September 1975 by tribal ordinance as the Northern Cheyenne Indian Action Program Incorporated, and was granted funding by the Indian Technical Assistance Center of the Bureau of Indian Affairs. The college gained accreditation in 1996 by the Northwest Association of Colleges and Schools.

COLLEGE OF MENOMINEE NATION

The Menominee Tribal Legislature chartered the College of Menominee Nation as an institution of higher education in March 1993. The North Central Association of Colleges and Schools granted full accreditation on August 7, 1998, making the college one of the youngest of the tribal colleges. The campus is located in Keshena, Wisconsin on the southern border of the Menominee Indian Reservation.

CROWNPOINT INSTITUTE OF TECHNOLOGY

The Crownpoint Institute of Technology (CIT) was originally established as the Navajo Skill Center in July 1979 for the purpose of providing vocational skills training. The institute has since evolved into a technical-vocational education center well known throughout the Southwest. In 1985, prompted by the school's expanding mission, the board of directors changed the institute's name to Crownpoint Institute of Technology. CIT is located on a seventy-acre campus in Crownpoint, New Mexico, on the eastern portion of the Navajo Nation.

DINÉ COLLEGE

The Navajo Nation established the "first" tribal college, Navajo Community College, in 1968. On May 17, 1997, the college name was changed to Diné College. In creating an institution of higher education, the Navajo Nation sought to encourage Navajo youth to become contributing members of the Navajo Nation and world society. Diné College, in Tsaile, Arizona, received accreditation by the North Central Association of Colleges and Schools in 1971. The educational philosophy of Diné College is Sa'ah Naaghai Bik'eh Hozhoon, the Diné traditional living system, which places human life in harmony with the natural world and the universe.

D-Q UNIVERSITY

D-Q University was founded in 1971 and is the only tribal college located in California. The university became accredited as a two-year college in 1977. The college derives its name from two important figures from Native history. The "D" stands for the name of the Great Peacemaker who inspired the founding of the Iroquois Confederacy; the full name symbolized by the "D" is used only in a religious context. The "Q" represents Quetzalcoatl, an Aztec prophet who symbolized the principles of wisdom and self-discipline.

FOND DU LAC TRIBAL AND COMMUNITY COLLEGE

Fond du Lac is unique in the United States as it is jointly a tribal and a state community college, part of the Minnesota State Colleges and Universities System. The college campus sits on top of a bluff overlooking Cloquet, a small community of 11,000 people in northern Minnesota. The Fond du Lac Reservation is part of the extensive Chippewa, or Ojibwa, Nation that once dominated much of the Great Lakes region. Unlike most reservations that are geographically isolated, Fond du Lac is close to the Lake Superior port city of Duluth, Minnesota.

FORT BELKNAP COLLEGE

Fort Belknap College was chartered by the Fort Belknap Community Council on November 8, 1984. In June 1993, Fort Belknap College received accreditation through the Northwest Association of Schools and Colleges. Fort Belknap is located on the Fort Belknap Reservation in north-central Montana, which is home of the Gros Ventre and the Assiniboine Tribes.

FORT BERTHOLD COMMUNITY COLLEGE

Fort Berthold Community College is located in New Town, North Dakota on the Fort Berthold Reservation of the Three Affiliated Tribes of the Arikara, Hidatsa, and Mandan peoples. The founding of Fort Berthold Community College was initiated on May 2, 1973, when the tribes decided that a locally based higher education institution was needed to train tribal members and act as a positive influence on retaining tribal culture. The college was granted accreditation status in February 1998.

FORT PECK COMMUNITY COLLEGE

Fort Peck Community College, in Poplar, Montana, is a tribally controlled community college chartered by the government of the Fort Peck Assiniboine and Sioux Tribes and officially chartered by the Fort Peck Tribal Executive Board in 1978. The main campus is located in Poplar, with an extension campus at Wolf Point. The college was granted full accreditation by the Northwest Association of Colleges and Schools in 1991.

HASKELL INDIAN NATIONS UNIVERSITY

The history and advancement of Haskell demonstrates how the goals of educating Native Americans have changed from advocating assimilation to advocating sovereignty and self-determination. In October 1993, Haskell changed its name from Haskell Indian Junior College to Haskell Indian Nations University after receiving accreditation to offer a bachelor of science degree in elementary education. Haskell is a cornerstone for Indian education with a long, rich tradition of generations of families utilizing this resource for their education. The university is located in Lawrence, Kansas, and supports and serves all federally recognized tribes.

INSTITUTE OF AMERICAN INDIAN ARTS

The Institute of American Indian Arts is the only institute of higher education in the world devoted solely to the study and practice of the artistic and cultural traditions of American Indian and Alaska Native peoples. Established by the Bureau of Indian Affairs (BIA) in 1962 as an "experimental" institution, IAIA has a long history and tradition of art education. The alumni and faculty list reads like a "Who's Who" in the Indian art world. IAIA was first accredited in 1984 by the North Central Association of Colleges and Schools and in 1986 by the National Association of Schools of Art and Design.

KEWEENAW BAY OJIBWA COMMUNITY COLLEGE

Keweenaw Bay Ojibwa Community College was chartered by the Keweenaw Bay Indian Community on July 12, 1975 in order to provide higher educational programs on the L'Anse Indian Reservation in Baraga, Michigan. The checkerboard reservation is located in northern Michigan on the shores of Lake Superior. Baraga is the tribe's headquarters. The L'Anse reservation was established in 1854 by treaty.

LAC COURTE OREILLES OJIBWA COMMUNITY COLLEGE

The Lac Courte Oreilles Ojibwa Tribe, recognizing its responsibilities for the higher education of tribal members, drafted a tribal resolution on August 20, 1982 establishing the Lac Courte Oreilles Ojibwa Community College to encourage the personal and intellectual development of students. The college draws its main body of students from the Lac Courte Oreilles Reservation, which is located in the northern lakes and woodlands region of Wisconsin.

LEECH LAKE TRIBAL COLLEGE

Leech Lake Tribal College was authorized by the Leech Lake Tribal Council with a tribal resolution in July 1990. From its inception, the college understood that its mission was to focus on the transmission of Anishinaabe language and culture, thus providing a space where Anishinaabe culture could be dominant. In addition, the college serves as a bridge to higher education for Leech Lake tribal members who may wish to continue studies at four-year institutions or in graduate school. The Leech Lake Reservation is located in north-central Minnesota.

LITTLE BIG HORN COLLEGE

Little Big Horn College is a public two-year community college chartered in January 1980 by the Crow Tribe. The college is located about sixty miles from Billings, Montana in Crow Agency, the capital of the Crow Indian Reservation. Little Big Horn College is dedicated to improving the lives of the people of the Crow Reservation by providing culturally sensitive education. The curriculum prepares students for degrees at four-year institutions as well as for work on the reservation.

LITTLE PRIEST TRIBAL COLLEGE

The Winnebago Tribe, or Ho-Chunk people of Nebraska, chartered Little Priest Tribal College in May 1996. The college's major focus is to provide a two-year associate degree and to prepare students to transfer and successfully complete a major at a four-year institution. The college is named after Chief Little Priest, the last true war chief of the Winnebago Tribe. The college is located on the Winnebago Reservation, which covers an area of 25,000 acres.

NEBRASKA INDIAN COMMUNITY COLLEGE

Nebraska Indian Community College began as the American Indian Satellite Community College in 1973, under a grant from the Fund for the Improvement of Post-Secondary Education for the Ho-Chunk, Omaha, and Santee Sioux Tribes in northeast Nebraska. The college is an Indian-focused institution offering a liberal arts and vocational education. In August 1986, the college gained accreditation from the North Central Association of Colleges and Schools.

NORTHWEST INDIAN COLLEGE

Northwest Indian College was founded in 1971 by the Lummi Indian Business Council as an aqua-cultural institute. Started on the Lummi Reservation, the institute was expected to train tribal members for work in fisheries. But as the economy diversified, additional courses and degrees were added. Designed to serve the educational needs of Indian people living in the Northwest, Northwest Indian College is the only accredited tribal college in Washington, Oregon, and Idaho. The Northwest Association of Colleges and Schools approved the college for accreditation in December 1993, and, in 1994, the college was designated as a Land Grant Institution.

OGLALA LAKOTA COLLEGE

Located on the Pine Ridge Indian Reservation in South Dakota, Oglala Lakota College stresses Lakota culture and tribal self-determination as a part of its mission. The Pine Ridge Reservation is the second largest reservation in the country. In fact, with the vastly dispersed campus, the Oglala Lakota College campus is larger than the state of Connecticut. On March 4, 1971, the Oglala Sioux Tribe exercised its sovereignty by chartering the Lakota Higher Education Center, one of the first tribal colleges. In 1978, the name of the college was changed to Oglala Sioux Community College, and the college became a candidate for accreditation. On June 20, 1983, Oglala Lakota College was officially accredited by the North Central Association of Colleges and Schools. Oglala Lakota College offers master's degrees.

SALISH KOOTENAI COLLEGE

Salish Kootenai College is located on the Flathead Indian Reservation, home of the Salish and Kootenai Tribes in the northwestern part of Montana. The campus sits at the base of the Mission Mountains. In 1976, The Confederated Salish and Kootenai Tribes created the college. Originally established to train tribal members for work in forestry, by 1984 Salish Kootenai College became the first regionally accredited Indian college in the Northwest and has received continued accreditation from the Northwest Association of Colleges and Schools.

SINTE GLESKA UNIVERSITY

One of the original tribal colleges, Sinte Gleska University is located on the Rosebud Sioux Reservation in south-central South Dakota. Sinte Gleska University was established in 1969 as Sinte Gleska College. In 1970, an all-Indian board of directors was established and, by the following year, the Rosebud Sioux Tribe granted a charter to Sinte Gleska. In 1983, Sinte Gleska was granted accreditation, making it the first tribally chartered college in the nation to become accredited at both the two-year and four-year levels. As of February 1992, Sinte Gleska College officially became Sinte Gleska University. The college offers master's degrees.

SISSETON WAHPETON COLLEGE

Sisseton Wahpeton College (FKA Sisseton Wahpeton Community College) was established on August 7, 1979 and granted accreditation in 1990. The college is located on the Lake Traverse Reservation in the northeastern corner of South Dakota and another portion of the reservation in southeastern North Dakota. The small college was also one of the first tribal colleges to establish an institute for the study and preservation of tribal culture. Arguing that Dakota is a culture distinct from Lakota, and thus has not been adequately studied, the college created the Institute for Dakota Studies in 1989. This center's mission is to teach, study, and preserve the tribe's unique history and traditions.

SI TANKA UNIVERSITY

Si Tanka University, formerly Cheyenne River Community College, is located in Eagle Butte, South Dakota on the Cheyenne River Sioux Reservation. The college was originally established April 4, 1973, through the action of the Cheyenne River Sioux Tribal Council. The college changed its name from Cheyenne River Community College to Si Tanka (Big Foot) College on July 12, 1999.

SITTING BULL COLLEGE

Sitting Bull College began as Standing Rock Community College on September 21, 1973. The tribal council changed the name to Sitting Bull College on March 6, 1996. The college is located on the Standing Rock Indian Reservation, which is uniquely located in both southern North Dakota and northern South Dakota. It was given full accreditation in 1984.

SOUTHWESTERN INDIAN POLYTECHNIC INSTITUTE (SIPI)

A school that would serve the Native American community was envisioned by the All Indian Pueblo Council in 1960, and through a ten-year collective effort involving other tribal leaders, public officials, and interested citizens, the construction finally commenced. Dedication ceremonies were held on August 21, 1971, and on September 16, 1971, SIPI officially opened its doors for classes. Located in Albuquerque, New Mexico, the institute has gained strong support from national corporations like Intel, Philips Semiconductors, and Sandia National Laboratory.

STONE CHILD COLLEGE

Stone Child College, in Rocky Boy, Montana, was chartered by the Chippewa-Cree Tribal Business Committee on May 17, 1984. Tribal leaders maintained that the establishment of a college remained necessary for the preservation and mainte-nance of the Chippewa-Cree culture and for the educational training of its tribal membership. Stone Child College is accredited by the Commission of the Northwest Association of Colleges and Schools. It is located at the Rocky Boy Agency on the Rocky Boy Reservation.

TURTLE MOUNTAIN COMMUNITY COLLEGE

Located ten miles from the Canadian border in North Dakota, Turtle Mountain Community College serves a tribe that is, in many ways, beating the odds. Although geographically isolated, the economy is relatively strong and cultural preservation remains a priority. The college was also one of the first tribal colleges to fully integrate traditional culture throughout the curriculum. The college is accredited by the North Central Association of Colleges and Schools and is one of the original six tribal colleges.

UNITED TRIBES TECHNICAL COLLEGE

United Tribes Technical College was founded in 1969 by an intertribal organization, the United Tribes of North Dakota Development Corporation. It is a nonprofit corporation, chartered by the state of North Dakota and operated by the five tribes, which are wholly or in part in North Dakota. These are the Three Affiliated Tribes of Fort Berthold, the Spirit Lake Tribe, the Sisseton-Wahpeton Sioux Tribe, the Standing Rock Sioux Tribe, and the Turtle Mountain Band of Chippewa. United Tribes Technical College applied for and was granted candidacy for accreditation status by the North Central Association of Colleges and Schools in 1978, and by 1982 was granted accreditation status as a vocational school.

WHITE EARTH TRIBAL AND COMMUNITY COLLEGE

The White Earth Reservation Tribal Council established the White Earth Tribal and Community College on September 8, 1997. The college is currently seeking accreditation through the North Central Association of Colleges and Schools. The attainment of independent accreditation as a two-year college is one of the primary goals of the college, which also hopes to offer four-year degrees in the future. The main campus of White Earth Tribal and Community College is located in Mahnomen, Minnesota.

The American Indian College Fund

America's tribal colleges and universities have been called "underfunded miracles" and "economic lifelines" for U.S. Indian reservations. There are thirty-two tribal colleges located throughout North America, each founded to fight high rates of poverty, educational failure, and cultural loss within Indian communities. Together they serve about 30,000 students from 250 tribes and indigenous groups from across the United States and Canada. The schools are mostly located on poor, isolated Indian reservations and operate in trailers, converted warehouses, and abandoned buildings. In fact, about 85 percent of tribal college students live at or below the poverty level.

Tribal colleges offer Indian students a unique form of higher education that includes both accredited academics and courses in Indian culture. The Carnegie Foundation for the Advancement of Teaching reported in 1997 that "the most significant development in American Indian communities since World War II was the creation of tribally controlled colleges."

The American Indian College Fund, based in Denver, Colorado, is a nonprofit organization founded in 1989 to raise desperately needed scholarship, endowment, and operating funds for these tribal colleges. With the support of corporations, foundations, and approximately 130,000 individuals, the College Fund has become the nation's largest provider of privately funded Indian scholarships. In addition, the College Fund also supports tribal college programs such as Indian teacher training, facilities construction, cultural preservation, and business development and technology.

The W.K. Kellogg Foundation

NATIVE AMERICAN HIGHER EDUCATION INITIATIVE

This publication was funded by the W.K. Kellogg Foundation as an ancillary project of the Native American Higher Education Initiative (NAHEI), the single largest foundation initiative to focus on tribal education.

The NAHEI was created under the doctrine that "Native Americans will shape their own futures and that of their communities through higher education that perpetuates tribal culture and honors the people, the land, the air, the water, and the animals that are essential for a healthy American and for world survival." Formally operating from 1995-2002, the Initiative sought to expand educational opportunity and access for Native American students, who, as a group, have the nation's lowest rates of educational success.

Focusing its work on tribal colleges and universities, as well as on other Native-serving institutions of higher education, the Initiative infused resources at a critical point in the development of tribal colleges, helping to meet the needs of tribal communities on many levels. It supported the creation of new degree programs, including dozens of new distance learning courses at Salish Kootenai College in Montana. In South Dakota, Oglala Lakota College established a new master's degree program in educational administration, the nation's first culturally based program for school administrators. Other colleges strengthened teacher training programs and linkages with K-12 schools. The Initiative also supported partnerships between tribal colleges and other universities. In Alaska, Native communities moved to establish a state higher education network. Brigham Young University-Hawaii created its first Hawaiian Studies degree program, which will be sustained with a newly established endowment fund.

All told, the W.K. Kellogg Foundation's investment in the Initiative totaled more than $30 million in grants to 50 different projects. The efforts fulfilled the mission of the Foundation, which was established in 1930 "to help people help themselves through the practical application of knowledge and resources to improve their quality of life and that of future generations."

Because tribal education is so entwined with Native culture and ways of community life, no one publication can tell the complete story. Still, the sacred stories in Real Indians—which are filled with personal inspiration, humor, and strength—are testament to the power of education to improve life for future generations.

About the Contributors

ANDREA MODICA's work has been published in three monographs, *Treadwell, Minor League,* and *Human Being,* as well as in magazines such as *Harper's, Mother Jones,* and *The New York Times Magazine.* After receiving her M.F.A. from the Yale School of Art in 1985, she was a professor in the art department at the State University of New York at Oneonta for thirteen years. She is the recipient of numerous grants, among them a 1994 Guggenheim Arts Fellowship and a 1990 Fulbright-Hays Research Grant. Modica's photographs are also included in numerous collections, including the Museum of Modern Art and the Metropolitan Museum of Art in New York, the George Eastman House in Rochester, New York, the National Museum of American Art in Washington, D.C., and the San Francisco Museum of Modern Art. She lives in Manitou Springs, Colorado, and is represented by Marilyn Cadenbach Associates in Cambridge, Massachusetts, the Edwynn Houk Gallery in New York, and the Catherine Edelman Gallery in Chicago.

SHERMAN ALEXIE is a Native American poet and author of fourteen books as well as a longtime supporter of the American Indian College Fund. His first book, *The Business of Fancydancing,* a collection of poetry and stories, was named a 1992 Notable Book of the Year. Alexie's first collection of short stories, *The Lone Ranger and Tonto Fistfight in Heaven,* published in 1994, was a citation winner for the PEN/Hemmingway Award for Best First Fiction as well as the basis for his first screenplay for the feature film, *Smoke Signals,* which premiered in 1998 at the Sundance Film Festival. *Smoke Signals* was the first feature film produced, written, and directed by American Indians. Among its numerous awards was the 1999 Christopher Award, given for works of art "which affirm the highest values of the human spirit." Alexie's numerous awards also include a PEN/Malamud Award from the PEN/Faulkner Foundation, a National Endowment for the Arts Poetry Fellowship, and a Lila Wallace-Readers Digest Writers' Award. A Spokane-Coeur d'Alene Indian from Wellpinit, Washington, Alexie currently resides in Seattle with his wife and two sons.

SUZETTE BREWER is a member of the Cherokee Nation from Stilwell, Oklahoma. She has served as communications program manager for the American Indian College Fund since 1999. Prior to joining the College Fund, she worked for a number of media organizations as a journalist and freelance writer, including the *Dallas Morning News, Oklahoma Today,* and the *Denver Post.* Ms. Brewer holds a bachelor of arts degree in political science from the University of Mississippi. She lives in Denver with her son.